Kangaroo

Animal
Series editor: Jonathan Burt

Kangaroo

John Simons

REAKTION BOOKS

Published by
REAKTION BOOKS LTD
33 Great Sutton Street
London EC1V 0DX, UK
www.reaktionbooks.co.uk

First published 2013
Copyright © John Simons 2013

Printed and bound in China

British Library Cataloguing in Publication Data
Simons, John, 1955–
    Kangaroo. – (Animal)
    1. Kangaroos. 2. Kangaroos – Symbolic aspects.
    3. Kangaroo hunting – Moral and ethical aspects – Australia.
    I. Title II. Series
    599.2'22-DC23

ISBN 978 1 86189 922 4

Contents

1 What is a Kangaroo?

Every non-human animal bears a burden placed on it by humans. For some, like camels, donkeys and horses, the burden is a literal one. For others, like spiders, snakes and crocodiles, it is one of fearfulness and, often, ignorance. For most, the burden is symbolic. The burden the kangaroo carries is that of strangeness. Perhaps no other animal has summed up the sense of otherness in the Western imagination as strongly as the kangaroo did when Australia was colonized. In 1862 the American poet Emily Dickinson invoked this association when she wrote a flirtatious and even suggestive letter to Thomas Higginson, an editor of the *Atlantic Monthly*, in which she refers to 'Myself the only Kangaroo among the Beauty'.[1]

This burden of strangeness continues today. When the writers of the 2009 popular television series *FlashForward* – which depicts a world in which the entire human race has suffered a 30-second loss of consciousness during which each person appears to have seen a piece of the future – wanted to find an image to demonstrate that the world really had been turned upside down, they showed a kangaroo insouciantly hopping down a city street strewn with the wreckage of crashed cars and enveloped in the smoke of burning aeroplanes. For them the kangaroo was not only an animal out of place in the catastrophic aftermath of the mass blackout but also the signifier of the change in the world order that the blackout might entail.

Yet for all their strangeness and for all this symbolic work that they do on our behalf kangaroos are not, like pandas or white tigers, rare. They are by no means confined to the island continent of Australia and their image is almost universally familiar. But although they are common and familiar, the strangeness they carry has meant that they are relatively unknown animals and, even in Australia, they are not well understood. Much of this book will concern itself with looking at the ways in which images of kangaroos are symbolically charged. But it will start with a review of the remarkable zoological features of the kangaroo, of its biological uniqueness and its amazingly adaptable life cycle. Perhaps if this aspect of the kangaroo were better understood, the burden of strangeness it bears might be justified beyond the mere fact of its novelty to non-Indigenous Australians and visitors to zoos and wildlife parks across the globe.

The genus *Macropus*, to which the kangaroo belongs, is highly differentiated and there are currently 65 known species.[2] I say known species very deliberately, since Australia and its neighbouring islands have a habit of delivering cryptozoological surprises. As recently as 1975 an entirely new species of kangaroo was found living within a short drive of the city of Melbourne. And in 1994 Professor Tim Flannery, now of Macquarie University and one of the most respected (and entertaining) authorities on kangaroos in the world, identified and described yet another new species, the dingiso (*Dendrolagus mbaiso* – a tree-kangaroo), in the forests of the Indonesian province of Papua. Kangaroos are related to two other families, the Hypsiprymnodontidae (represented only by a curious little creature, the musky rat-kangaroo, that lives in North Queensland) and the Potoroidae (potoroos,

The grizzled tree-kangaroo (*Dendrolagus inustus*), from John Gould, *The Mammals of Australia* (1863).

bettongs and two rat-kangaroos). Within the Macropodidae family we find kangaroos, tree-kangaroos, various types of wallaby, quokkas, oolacuntas, monjons, warabis, tammars, wallaroos, euros and pademelons. But what most people mean when they say kangaroo and what, I think, they imagine, are the four large

The eastern (formerly great) grey kangaroo (*Macropus giganteus*, ex *M. major*), from Gould, *The Mammals of Australia* (1863).

species: the red kangaroo (*Macropus rufus*), the eastern grey kangaroo (*Macropus giganteus*), the western grey kangaroo (*Macropus fuliginosus*) and the antilopine kangaroo (*Macropus antilopinus*). The red kangaroo (which is the biggest, growing up to 2 metres in height) lives in the centre of the continent; the eastern and

The western
grey (formerly
West-Australian
great) kangaroo
(*Macropus
fuliginosus*, ex
M. ocydromus),
from Gould,
*The Mammals
of Australia* (1863).

MACROPUS OCYDROMUS, *Gould*

western greys live in the more fertile areas in the east and west of
the continent respectively; and the antilopine kangaroo has a
range in similar areas of the far north.

Red kangaroos have a tail which is over 1 metre in length and
this serves as a counterbalance because they cannot walk but only

The red (formerly great red) kangaroo (*Macropus rufus*, ex *Osphranter rufus*), from Gould, *The Mammals of Australia* (1863).

hop. This they do with amazing power and can clear 2 metres in height during a single bound, with which they may travel as far as 10 metres. Their top speed is 50 kilometres per hour and they can cruise at 20 kilometres per hour all day if necessary. This stamina and speed was, I think, one of the features that made them so attractive and, therefore, so vulnerable to hunting for

The antilopine kangaroo, formerly red wallaroo (*Macropus antilopinus*, ex *Osphranter antilopinus*), from Gould, *The Mammals of Australia* (1863).

sport, in the early days of European settlement. The eastern grey is similarly athletic and will reach speeds of up to 60 kilometres per hour with individual bounds 3 metres in height and covering 8 metres at a time. The most distinctive feature of the western grey is the strong smell of curry that emanates from the males. This is so pungent that they are commonly known as 'stinkers'.

Map showing red
kangaroo range.

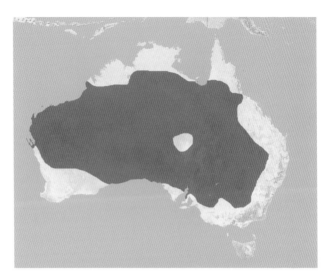

Antilopine
kangaroo range.

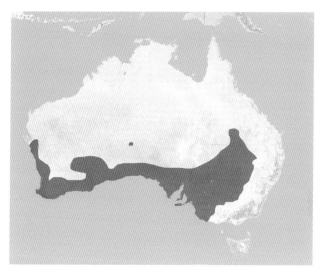

Western grey
kangaroo range.

Eastern grey
kangaroo range.

The red kangaroo (*Macropus rufus*).

Kangaroos and their relatives have a significant heritage that can be traced in the record of palaeontology. Before and at the time of the arrival of the peoples who became Indigenous Australians, the continent was inhabited by a remarkably varied and surprising collection of megafauna. From the fossil record these were widely distributed across the continent with some notable deposits at the Wellington Caves in New South Wales, Naracoorte Caves in South Australia and the Thylacoleo, Mammoth and Tight Entrance Caves in Western Australia, as well as at King's Creek in Queensland, Lake Callabonna in South Australia, the Western District Lakes of Victoria and Cuddie Springs in New South Wales. Excavations at Lancefield in Victoria suggest an extinction date between 40,000 and 50,000 years ago, and stone artefacts found with the fossil deposits show clearly that humans coexisted with the megafauna.

The megafauna included such exotic creatures as *Thylacoleo carnifex* (the marsupial lion) and *Diprotodon optatum*, a kind of

The eastern grey kangaroo (*Macropus giganteus*).

The western grey kangaroo (*Macropus fuliginosus*).

The antilopine kangaroo (*Macropus antilopinus*).

wombat as big as a female Indian elephant. But there was a massive variety of macropods: for example, the giant, short-faced kangaroos (*Simosthenurus occidentalis*), the terrifying carnivorous *Ekaltadeta ima* (the killer rat-kangaroo) and the *Balbaroo fangaroo*, with its exotic dentition. There were fourteen species of short-faced kangaroos alone and, to give some idea of their

A museum palaeontologist standing next to an early reconstruction of the giant kangaroo (*Palorchestes azael*) in the Australian Museum, Sydney.

size, the largest, *Procoptodon goliah*, weighed over 200 kilograms and could reach 3 metres or more from the ground. This would make it, at a minimum, twice the size of the biggest kangaroo extant today in terms of weight and about half as tall again as a full-grown male red kangaroo. Almost as big was *Macropus titan*, an ancestor of the grey kangaroo. The banded

hare-wallaby (*Lagostrophus fasciatus*) is a small kangaroo that
is the sole living representative of these prehistoric giants. It has
been extinct on the mainland since 1963 but now thrives, as a
dwarf version of its gigantic ancestors, in small colonies on
Faure, Bernier and Dorre islands off the coast of Western Australia. These animals became extinct during the time of the early
settlement of Australia by its first people and the scientific evidence suggests that it was their impact as hunters and managers
of the landscape through clearance by fire that hastened, if not

'Another view of this 9-ft baby': a really big red kangaroo, 1932.

caused, the extinction not only of the giant macropods but of all the megafauna.

This thesis has caused dire offence to many Indigenous Australians, who see custodianship of country and nature as one of the most significant features of their culture and one which contrasts favourably with the poor environmental record of European and other settlers. As they point out, the first peoples made a good job of managing Australia for 50,000 years or more while the European and Asian colonists degraded the

environment in only two short centuries. This is a powerful
point which has much merit and is not, I think, particularly
diminished by the case of megafauna extinction. It is the case
that Indigenous Australian stories and art offer the world probably the only record of what it was like for human beings to
coexist with megafauna and this constitutes a considerable
contribution to world knowledge. It is true also that the most
successful evolutionary strategy for Australian mammals has
been selection for small size, so the associated long-term logic
was that the megafauna would die out to be replaced by the
smaller forms extant today. The intervention of humans would
at most only have accelerated an inevitable process that was
probably completed with the arrival in Australia of the dingo
some 6,000 years ago.

In addition, Indigenous rock art depicting kangaroos and
kangaroo hunts has enabled modern scientists and conservationists to understand the history of kangaroo ecology by
enabling them to plot the distribution of different species in the

past. Recently, interviews with the Bininj Kunwok people of western Arnhem Land has revealed extensive knowledge of the behaviour and ecology of four rock wallaby species (*Petrogale brachyotis*, *Petrogale concinna*, *Macropus bernardus* and *Macropus robustus*), which significantly supplements and complements existing scientific understanding of the animal with regard to diet, predation, breeding patterns and habitat preferences. Most Indigenous people would argue that Indigenous knowledge of Australian animals is likely to add to conventionally acquired scientific study and should not be neglected.[3]

Indigenous Australian hunters carrying a dead kangaroo, photographed *c.* 1942.

So what are the features that have made the kangaroo so successful and enabled it to survive in large numbers in relatively inhospitable environments, even in times of severe drought such as much of Australia has recently experienced? And why might it be in Australia's interests to promote kangaroo numbers in

Indigenous Australian rock art at Nourlangie Rock, Burrunguy, Northern Territories.

order to develop a meat industry and as a conservation measure? Indeed, why might it be in the interests of the entire human race to promote the growth of kangaroo populations?

In the first place kangaroos have a remarkable digestive system. They live almost exclusively on grass and have developed a dentition that enables them to cope with such highly abrasive foodstuffs without wearing out their teeth. Like ruminants, kangaroos have a multiple stomach. In kangaroos it is divided into three parts and this enables them to digest their tough food by allowing microorganisms living in the forestomach to work on the fibre contained in the grass. Kangaroos indulge in a cud-chewing activity known as mercyism, but this appears not to have the same function as cud chewing in other ruminants and seems to be designed more as a further aid to digestion by enabling saliva to play its part in the process of breaking down the grass.

While kangaroos are supremely well adapted for nourishing themselves in the sometimes harsh environments of Australia, they are even better adapted for reproduction. The reproductive cycle of kangaroos is complex: they have the unique property of being able to suspend or abort a pregnancy and also to become pregnant while still nursing a joey (the usual name for a young kangaroo) in the pouch. This enables them to reproduce at a rate that suits the specific environmental and climactic conditions that obtain at any time: they can self-manage the population in order to exploit times of great abundance by maximizing reproduction and see out times of drought and famine by keeping numbers low. A female kangaroo might have a young joey hopping along beside her and still feeding from her milk, a baby in the pouch and a foetus in suspended animation in the womb. She is able to produce different kinds of milk for the different stages of the joey's development (milk for the early stage has a high sugar and low fat content, and as the joey develops the proportions gradually change in favour of fat and protein) and she can control the sex of her babies. She has three vaginas: two

Kangaroo just after birth.

Newborn kangaroo feeding.

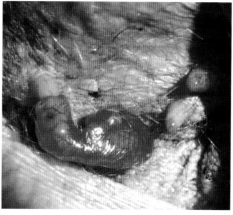

lateral, which are used to convey sperm, and one medial, which acts as the birth canal.

In a red kangaroo, pregnancy lasts about 40 days and the young kangaroo is only 10 millimetres long at birth. It then spends five minutes crawling through its mother's fur until it finds her pouch and, clambering in, attaches itself to a nipple. It will use only this nipple until it is weaned; any further joeys will have a nipple of their own from which to feed. The mother will soon breed again and will hold the new foetus in suspension. If the joey in the pouch is lost for any reason she will activate the pregnancy and soon repeat the cycle. This astonishing ability means that kangaroos can survive the vicissitudes of climate. They live between ten and fifteen years in the wild and can survive longer, up to twenty years and maybe beyond, in captivity.

Kangaroos have other physiological features that enable them to thrive in Australia. They have exceptionally strong jaws

Wallaby joey
in pouch.

and the jawbone has a deep hole in it into which the main cheek muscle passes and to which it is attached. This gives great biting power and suggests an evolutionary past in which kangaroos ate foods that they needed to break into. Second, the foot of a kangaroo is constructed of a number of bones joined by facets rather than mobile joints, and in some species the bones have fused together. This seems to have been driven by a change from tree dwelling to ground dwelling but is now marvellously adapted for hopping. Finally, in common with other marsupials, the male's penis is situated behind the scrotum and so is long and s-shaped in order to bypass the hanging testicles. Interestingly, this is not a specific adaptation but rather a failure to evolve from an arrangement that was once common to all mammals including humans.

These extraordinary features ought to explain both our enduring fascination with the kangaroo and its strangeness, for perhaps anything that can survive the occasionally extreme Australian climate is strange. The biological uniqueness of the kangaroo ought also to explain why we should value it highly. But the animal has other values, and these are especially significant for Australia. The first is that the kangaroo is soft-footed and so does very little damage to the land on which it moves and grazes. This means that the fertility of the land is, arguably, not compromised by kangaroo grazing and needs minimal recovery time when compared with grazing by hard-footed animals such as cattle and sheep. In addition, the kangaroo's adaptation to the Australian environment means that it does not require special arrangements for feeding and watering. All kangaroos, except the odd pet or zoo or wildlife park animal, are free-range and live wild. They are culled via hunting, not farming (a thing not understood by many Australians), and essentially look after themselves.

The final biological features worth noting are the digestive adaptations of kangaroos, which mean that they do not produce any of the greenhouse gas methane. The flatulence of cattle and sheep produces between 250 and 300 litres of methane per animal per day. All this adds up to an annual total of greenhouse gas emissions equivalent to about 66 per cent of that produced by the entire Australian transport system or about 11 per cent of Australia's total greenhouse gas emissions. It is unlikely that the Australian livestock economy would ever move lock, stock and barrel towards kangaroo management, but it appears that other animals can be inoculated with the bacteria from the kangaroo's gut and thus acquire some of the greater efficiency which enables the kangaroo to digest so much more of its food. Kangaroos could thus not only help to reduce greenhouse gas emissions but also help solve the problem of feeding the animals that will form the food supply of a growing global population. Dr Ming Wei of the University of Queensland has found that commensal bacteria from eastern grey kangaroos have significant

The crescent nail-tail wallaby (*Onychongalea lunata*), from John Gould, *The Mammals of Australia* (1863).

success in preventing the spread of cancerous tumours in mice when injected into the bloodstream, and he is preparing to begin full clinical trials. Trials are also under way to investigate the apparent value of kangaroo-based products in the treatment of skin cancer.[4]

Although this book will focus on the four main kinds of large kangaroo, it is worth looking briefly at three of the minor species since this will give the reader a much better idea of the specificity and adaptations of the genus *Macropus*.

The tammar wallaby (*Macropus eugenii*) is a small kangaroo that lives on islands off the coast of South Australia and Western Australia. It is found in very significant populations on Kangaroo Island. This little animal (which is about the size of a large domestic cat) has a very specific habitat and this specificity means that three subspecies have evolved. The first is *Macropus eugenii eugenii*, which lived on the South Australian mainland but has been extinct there since 1925 due to the depredations of introduced cats and foxes. It does, however, live as an

Map showing tammar wallaby range.

introduced species (and is seen as a huge pest) on Kawau Island
in New Zealand. Since 2004 there has been a re-introduction of
the New Zealand animals into Innes National Park on the Yorke
Peninsula, which is predator-free and a part of the tammar's
former mainland Australian range. Then there are *Macropus
eugenii derbianus* from Western Australia and *Macropus eugenii
decres*. *Macropus eugenii decres* forms the large Kangaroo Island
population and members of this subspecies are also known as
darma or dama wallabies.

The tammar has an important role to play in kangaroo history
(and indeed Australian history), as it was first seen in 1628 by
the survivors of the horrific shipwreck and subsequent mas-
sacres that befell the Dutch ship *Batavia*.[5] Here a rogue officer

The nabarlek, formerly the little rock wallaby (*Petrogale concinna*), from Gould, *The Mammals of Australia* (1863).

took advantage of the captain's absence – he had gone for help in one of those epic open-boat voyages that pepper the history of European expansion into the Pacific – to set up a nightmare mini-state based on sexual exploitation, slavery and murder on what are now the Houtman Abrolhos Islands just off the coast of Western Australia and where a population of tammars lived and still live. By the time the rescue ship arrived he and his henchmen had murdered at least 110 of the original survivors. The next year it was formally recorded by Pelsaert (the original captain and hero of the *Batavia* disaster) in his account of the unfortunate expedition. So the tammar was the first kangaroo (and maybe the first Australian mammal) recorded as being sighted by Europeans – although of course Portuguese explorers who were almost certainly making clandestine visits to Australia 100 years earlier may well have seen other examples including, possibly, kangaroos. Tammars are proving significant in another way too, since current experiments are isolating an antibiotic from tammar milk that appears to be 100 times more effective than penicillin and capable of killing *Salmonella*.

The quokka (*Setonix brachyurus*), or *gwaga* to the local Nyungar people, is another largely island-based macropod and lives especially on Rottnest Island, just off the coast of Perth in Western Australia, where it has survived and thrived due to the absence of foxes and cats. It is smaller than the tammar and is more like a domestic cat in size. In spite of their largely island habitat, quokkas are rare animals and, being of a very gentle and curious disposition, often put themselves in danger by approaching dogs and humans. They are protected by punitive fines; just touching a quokka will cost you AUD$300. Like the tammar, the quokka plays an important role in early kangaroo history. It was first seen by the Dutch in 1658 and again, more famously, in 1696 when de Vlamingh assumed the animals he saw to be rats and named the island on which they were seen *Rattenest* (Rat Nest). This zoological inaccuracy seems remarkable to us, but how was he to know what these odd little animals were? This was a persistent problem for the early European visitors to Australia.

The quokka (*Setonix brachyurus*), a relation of the kangaroo and wallaby.

The quokka, formerly Gilbert's rat-kangaroo (*Setonix brachyurus*, ex *Halmaturus brachyurus*), from Gould, *The Mammals of Australia* (1863).

There is also a quokka colony on the mainland at Two Peoples Bay. This is of interest as here the quokkas live with the very rare marsupial Gilbert's potoroo. This had been assumed to be extinct for 115 years – the last known specimen was described in 1879 – until 1994 when one was found and initially thought to be a small quokka. Subsequently, some 50 potoroos have been identified and they are being urgently made the centre of a conservation programme. It appears that they have always cohabited with the quokka, and the naturalist John Gilbert presented the first European description of this tiny macropod in 1840. In *The Mammals of Australia* John Gould remarked (citing a letter he had receieved from John Gilbert when the animal was first identified) that 'natives will kill them [potoroos and quokkas] in immense numbers . . . in a few hours'. Gould named

the potoroo in memory of Gilbert who was killed in 1845 when Indigenous Australians attacked the camp of the explorer Leichardt with whom Gilbert was travelling.

Oolacunta is the Indigenous Australian name for the almost mythical desert rat-kangaroo (*Caloprymnus campestris*). This small creature was first described and drawn from specimens sent to John Gould in 1843. It then disappeared from the record. In 1931 what looked like oolacuntas were sighted by John Finlayson of the Appamunna Station and an expedition under the experienced naturalist Hedley Herbert Finlayson was sent to find some on behalf of the South Australian Museum in Adelaide. Finlayson and his colleagues searched on horseback and found what looked like an oolacunta. They chased it and, to their amazement, it outran their horses (three had to give up from

Gilbert's potoroo (*Potorous gilbertii*, ex *Hypsiprymnus gilberti*), from Gould, *The Mammals of Australia* (1863).

Henry Richter's depiction of the desert rat-kangaroo or oolacunta (*Caloprymnus campestris*), from Gould, *The Mammals of Australia* (1863).

exhaustion) for 12 miles, at which point it died. It was confirmed to be an oolacunta and in the weeks that followed Finlayson's expedition collected another seven specimens as well as a mother and baby which were extracted from their lair by Finlayson's Indigenous Australian guides, who claimed that the animal had once been plentiful in the area. Over the weeks Finlayson's team saw enough of the creatures to deduce that, far from being extinct, it was relatively plentiful and sightings continued into the late 1930s when the animal appears to have become scarce, if not extinct, again. However, there were sporadic sightings into the 1950s and one or two speculative encounters in the late 1970s. Since then it appears to have, yet again, become extinct. It survives in a wonderful illustration by John Gould and an evocative and grainy photograph by Finlayson. It now has its own Facebook page. Whether it is really extinct or living in good numbers within a short drive of Adelaide, only time will tell.

After all, a specimen of the mountain pygmy possum (*Burramys parvus*), which had previously been assumed extinct and was known only from fossils, was found perfectly well and living the high life in a ski lodge on Victoria's Mount Hotham in 1966. While it is still designated as endangered, it is common in the small area of its currently known range. So the oolacunta may well be found again – perhaps in a casino.

As the story of these three rare species shows, the various kinds of macropods have different conservation statuses. Some are vulnerable, some are endangered and some – by far the largest group – are secure. In the secure group we find the red and grey kangaroos which, as I have suggested, are really the archetype for everyone's idea of what a kangaroo should look like and what it should do.

But this was not always the case. At the beginning of the twentieth century numbers of some of the now-common types of kangaroo were falling due to a mixture of poor land management practices (from the point of view of suitability for the Australian environment), exclusion of Indigenous people from

The desert rat-kangaroo or oolacunta, photographed in 1932.

their traditional country and overhunting. In some areas this overhunting was almost on the scale of the American assault on the bison or passenger pigeon. In other places kangaroo numbers rose so it is not possible to put together a neat argument that suggests that the impact of European and Asian settlement was wholly bad for kangaroo populations. Population change varied from region to region. In addition, the remarkable adaptation of the kangaroo to the Australian environment, indeed to almost any environment where reasonable levels of grass are available, means that after times of severe environmental stress and population depletion numbers bounce back remarkably quickly.

Although kangaroo numbers in the main species are secure, there is plenty of evidence to suggest that, overall, numbers were significantly higher prior to and during the first century of European and Asian settlement and that hunting of kangaroos by Indigenous Australian peoples and predation by dingoes probably had only the most marginal effect, if any, on population

The yellow-footed rock wallaby (*Petrogale xanthopus*), from Gould, *The Mammals of Australia* (1863).

numbers. Indeed, when Indigenous people saw the ruthless efficiency of European hunting using hounds they quickly adopted the practice where they could.

Estimates of early kangaroo numbers are, to some extent, necessarily based on anecdotal evidence. In the early years of New South Wales, Queensland, Western Australia, Victoria and Tasmania kangaroos were clearly abundant. In 1794 just one hunter with six dogs working from Parramatta – which is now the geographical centre of the greater Sydney conurbation – could secure 300 pounds of kangaroo meat per week. Every account from both the settlers and the explorers of this period and into the 1830s speaks of vast mobs of kangaroos. However, in Tasmania the kangaroo was forced into the interior by 1808 and, by 1850, overhunting for meat had caused serious questions to be asked about the continued viability of the Tasmanian kangaroo population. Colonists in Queensland were also recording significant falls in the kangaroo population by the late 1840s. Although Tim Flannery has suggested that the red kangaroo

The Tasmanian padelemon, formerly Tasmanian wallaby (*Thylogale billardierii*, ex *Halmaturus billardieri*), from Gould, *The Mammals of Australia* (1863).

The Tasmanian padelemon, from Gould, *The Mammals of Australia* (1863).

John Skinner Prout,
*Cascade Falls,
Hobart*, c. 1853,
oil on canvas.

may well have been rarer in the nineteenth century than it is now, the weight of evidence appears to suggest otherwise.[6]

In the earlier colonial period various attempts were made to protect the growing pastoral industry by controlling kangaroo numbers. In 1879 New South Wales proposed a Marsupials Destruction Bill which came into force as the Pastures and Stock Protection Act in 1880. This was aimed, *inter alia*, at kangaroos, wallaroos, wallabies and pademelons. One estimate has determined that about 21.4 million kangaroos and wallabies were killed under the provisions of the Act between 1881 and 1900. Other Australian states followed suit. Under Queensland's Marsupial Destruction Act as many as 27 million marsupials died between 1877 and 1930. This seems to have frightened people and by 1934 the New South Wales Pastures Protection Act excluded marsupials from the list of fair game, and various subsequent legislation has increased the legal protection afforded to many marsupial species – interestingly, the first ever animal

The Tasmanian bettong (*Bettongia cuniculus*), from Gould, *The Mammals of Australia* (1863).

protection legislation in Australia, the 1866 New South Wales Game Protection Act, offered a legal umbrella only to introduced mammals and native game birds.

The best estimates of total kangaroo numbers in the pre-colonial era put the population between 100 and 200 million. Today, the three main types of large kangaroos (the red, eastern grey and western grey) are estimated to number some 57 million and this number shows no sign of falling for these kinds of kangaroos. The significant drop in numbers from the colonial period is the result of a combination of hunting, predation by introduced animals, collisions with motor vehicles and changes in land use especially for the pastoral industry. However, the growth of the trade in kangaroo products, especially meat and leather, appears, at least in part, to account for the stability of the population at a sustainably high level, and the culling of wild kangaroos (they are never farmed) in relatively large numbers seems only to stimulate population growth.

About 7 million reds, eastern greys and western greys may be taken in any one year under a state-by-state and species-by-

species quota system with the actual numbers culled usually tracking beneath the maximum quota. The three large species represent roughly 95 per cent of the total quota for legal culling of macropods across Australia. The cull is regulated by a code of

Edward Roper, *A Boomer Held Up*, c. 1850, oil on paper.

Kangaroo hunting on a promotional postcard of *c.* 1903: 'The dog cannot be induced to again tackle the "Old Man"'.

No. 3. KANGAROO HUNTING, AUSTRALIA

The dog cannot be induced to again tackle the "Old Man."

COMPLIMENTS OF SINGER SEWING MACHINES

COPYRIGHT

practice first formulated in 1985. The number presently culled may be compared with the roughly 750,000 pelts that were put on the fur market every year in the early 1920s when there was some real concern about the sustainability of kangaroo numbers, even among the big species. In his influential book about animal introductions into Australia *They All Ran Wild* (the title says it all), Eric Rolls asked if the kangaroo was a 'Pest or Valuable Producer' and, in the chapter with this title, argued that numbers were plentiful in the early days of European settlement but then fell as large-scale hunting became more common. Rolls concluded (this was in 1969) that the future of the red kangaroo at any rate would be best assured by commercial exploitation, an argument that has resurfaced periodically ever since, though it is still far from winning the day – assuming that it should.[7]

This is a controversial area, of course. In Australia itself kangaroos are not especially well understood by the general population – which is overwhelmingly urban in character – and although the consumption of kangaroo meat is on the rise (this will be dealt with in more detail later) many Australians are reluctant to eat the national symbol, and older Australians often associate it with dog meat and believe that it is worm-ridden, which it is not. South Australians and Western Australians are much more likely to eat kangaroo meat than their compatriots in Queensland, while in New South Wales kangaroo eating remains a minority pursuit. Claims for the benefits of kangaroo meat include reference to its ultra-low fat content (2 per cent or less) and its very high concentrations of conjugated linoleic acid, which appears to have anti-carcinogenic properties as well as contributing to the reduction of obesity and atherosclerosis. There is a current vogue for 'kangatarianism' – a diet which excludes all meat products except kangaroo on the grounds that the meat is healthier, that it is more humane to cull free-roaming animals than it is to produce animals for consumption and that eating only locally produced food offers significant environmental benefits. Even so, kangaroo meat accounts for only about 2 per cent of the total meat consumption of Australia. As long ago as 1988 Professor Gordon Grigg advocated a long-term shift from traditional stock animals to kangaroos, with prices maintained at a level sufficiently high to make this shift commercially attractive to farmers as a method for solving the increasingly obvious environmental problems caused by the pressure put on both land and water resources by ever-growing herds of sheep and cattle.[8]

In Europe, where kangaroos and the nature of Australia are even less well understood, there are significant animal welfare campaigns against Australian kangaroo culling led by major

Kangaroo burger
at an outdoor
event in New
South Wales,
2008.

public figures such as Sir Paul McCartney and Dame Judi Dench. It is true that Australia has some of the least comprehensive and least enforced animal welfare laws in the world, especially where the management of animals for agricultural purposes is concerned. It is also undoubtedly true that, as in any industry based on the slaughter of animals for human food, there will be many acts of cruelty. However, while campaigning for the regulation of the kangaroo industry to promote the welfare of the free-range animals is one thing, it is an entirely different thing to campaign against it on the grounds that it might drive kangaroos into extinction. The main species of kangaroo are not rare and numbers are clearly going the other way, with kangaroos inhabiting, in some form or other, virtually all of Australia as well as large areas of Indonesia and Papua New Guinea. In addition, there are introduced kangaroo populations in New Zealand and colonies – some introduced, some feral runaways from zoos – in several European countries and elsewhere.

Nevertheless, kangaroo culling and conservation continues to stir strong passions among Australians. In 1988 the federal government commissioned and published a significant report on the kangaroo industry which made some effort to strike a balance between the need for conservation, the need for protection of agricultural land and the opportunities the kangaroo offered to the food industry.[9] More recently the Think Tank for Kangaroos (THINKK) at the University of Technology Sydney has published a series of reports that cast grave doubts on increasingly established ideas about population management, conservation, the viability of the kangaroo meat industry and the quality of kangaroo meat. In particular, THINKK reports draw attention to the allegedly large number of joeys that are killed or left to die a miserable death as collateral damage in the shooting of adult female kangaroos. The reports also point out the near impossibility for hunters to comply with the regulations that stipulate the animals should be killed by a shot to the brain and show how figures that suggest that up to 96 per cent are shot in this way may well mask a much more complex and less comfortable reality.[10]

Ogilby's jerboa-kangaroo (*Bettongia ogilbyi*), from Gould, *The Mammals of Australia* (1863).

A kangaroo hunter with his night's catch, 1998.

THINKK reports also show that Grigg's arguments for the benefits of an increased kangaroo harvest and the development of a kangaroo industry have not been fulfilled and that although the kangaroo industry has grown significantly and is now worth well over AUD$270 million per year and employs more than 4,000 people (mostly in the economically fragile and demographically vulnerable rural areas of remote Australia), this growth has not been achieved by any significant reduction in the beef and lamb industries. THINKK points out that selective culling may have long-term detrimental effects on the diversity of the kangaroo gene pool and lead to catastrophic population collapses as are sometimes seen in commercial fisheries. In addition, THINKK scientists have argued convincingly that the aim of developing a viable and prosperous kangaroo industry and the aim of managing kangaroos to reduce their impact on other kinds of agriculture exist in an irresoluble tension that creates crude solutions to complex problems and over-heavy weighting of very delicate environmental balances.

Kangaroo trying to escape an Australian Defence Force cull, 2009.

Although culling goes on more or less continuously, it does not feature as an especially controversial item in Australia except within the circles of animal welfare and environmental activism. Interesting exceptions to this are the large-scale culls periodically conducted by the Australian Defence Force, particularly on its bases in Victoria and the Australian Capital Territory. These seem to attract an unusual degree of public concern and opprobrium far beyond activist groups. I suspect that what we see here is the 'not in my name' phenomenon. In other words, people are more or less comfortable with the idea of culling for commercial purposes as part of a recognized agricultural industry, but less happy when the state takes a hand.[11]

The perceived strangeness of the kangaroo started with the very first British encounters with them on the *Endeavour* voyage of discovery and colonization between 1768 and 1771. Other Europeans, notably the Dutch and French but also, much earlier, the Portuguese and Spanish, had met, described and eaten

Albino kangaroo,
c. 1944.

macropods long before what is often mistakenly thought to be
the British discovery of Australia. In 1770 Captain James Cook
observed what were probably eastern grey kangaroos in northern Queensland and asked what they were called. The Guugu
Yimidhirr people told him *gangurru*, because that is the Guugu

Yimidhirr word for the particular kind of kangaroo they were looking at at the time (importantly, it is not a generic name for any old kangaroo). However, the word was not collected again until 1972. There may have been a number of reasons for this, ranging from lack of curiosity about Indigenous languages to the totemic nature of Indigenous culture in which words relating to the totems of deceased people may well disappear from the language for a time. But whatever the reason, the myth has emerged that the word 'kangaroo' means 'I don't know', and although the mystery was solved nearly 40 years ago this fallacious (and somewhat disrespectful) notion has proved remarkably tenacious.

In 2008 a BBC television documentary about Captain Cook featured an interview with a self-styled Aboriginal historian who, I suspect, was more prized by the director for his exotic appearance than for his knowledge. He actually repeated the 'I don't know' myth and, what is worse, repeated it as if it were related to the Darug or Gadigal people of the Sydney area, who spoke an entirely different language and never used the word *gangurru* anyway. Cook saw the same kind of kangaroos in Tasmania in 1777 but there is no record of a native term for them from that encounter. When the First Fleet arrived at Botany Bay in 1788, Governor Philip was prudently armed with Banks's Australian vocabulary but, of course, the local people had no more understanding of Guugu Yimidhirr than Philip had of Mongolian. In a curious form of linguistic colonization, the Guugu Yimidhirr word became imposed on the country of the Bediagal, Birrabirragal, Borogegal, Boromedegal, Buruberongal, Darramurragal, Gadigal, Gahbrogal, Gamaragal, Gameyagal, Garigal, Gayamaygal, Gwengal, Wallumedegal and Wangal, who between them spoke Darginung, Darug, Dharawhal, Gundungurra and Guringai (these are just the peoples and languages of Sydney Cove – there

were many more just inland). In fact, there is even some evidence that the Indigenous peoples of the Sydney area actually assumed that 'kangaroo' was an English word, possibly referring to horses which they had not seen before some arrived with the early colonists. And, of course, in New South Wales, it is the red not the grey kangaroo that predominates, so the term 'kangaroo' (which appears to apply to a very specific kind of kangaroo) was not accurate in any way.[12]

The accepted technical term *Macropus* was first coined by George Shaw in 1790, but the first attempts to fit kangaroos into a Latinate taxonomy were made by German scientists who were working from the image and descriptions in the published version of the account of Cook's voyage. In 1776 Müller suggested *Mus canguru*, in 1777 Zimmerman assayed *Yerboa gigantea* and in the same year Erxleben entered the lists with *Jaculus giganteus*. One can see here how the naming of an animal is so important if we are to have any chance of understanding it. The German names are clearly striving to find a relationship between the kangaroo and other known animals. Their attempts sum up the predicament of those who, faced with an entirely new continent, had to modify the entirety of existing scientific knowledge. As Joseph Banks wrote in his journal: 'To compare it to any European animal would be impossible as it has not the least resemblance to any one I have seen.'

In encountering the kangaroo Indigenous Australians found a rich source of food and, in addition, a companion who would bear many stories and take on some very important cultural values. Some of these cultural meanings are not available to anyone but the members of those groups within which the inner significance of the stories is shared. But from the earliest times of the settlement of Australia, between 40,000 and 50,000 years ago, we encounter rock art images of kangaroos and in the modern period the kangaroo in various forms plays a most important role in the Aboriginal art movement.

When Europeans first met the kangaroo they also encountered a source of food, although they did not exploit it as they might have done. They also met an animal that summed up Australia in all its strengths, weaknesses and contradictions. Their representations of this new arrival in their imaginations depicted all their hopes and fears. The remainder of this book will explore those hopes and fears and the ways in which representations of kangaroos embodied them in different ways. Perhaps, though, it would be true to say that the kangaroo is really only just beginning to be discovered by non-Indigenous Australia. Fortunately, this discovery is taking place while there are still plenty of kangaroos to enjoy and learn from. They still have much to teach us about the environment, how to protect it and how to live in it and with it. The situation for so many other Australian animals has, sadly, been very different.

Indigenous
Australian bark
painting, 1960.

The dusky wallaby (*Thylogale brunii*, ex *Dorcopsis bruni*), from Gould, *The Mammals of Australia* (1863).

This book is about the meaning of kangaroos in Australia and beyond. It is also about the ways in which animals can be turned into symbols, which are often multi-layered and complex. Above all, it will argue that the kangaroo is not an Australian animal at all, but an English invention that arrived in Botany Bay on that January day in 1788 – less than 24 hours ahead of the

French mission that might have given Australia a very different history – and hopped onshore in the pages of the officers' copies of the journals of Banks and Cook, alongside the convicts, Royal Marines and civil servants from whose efforts a new country would eventually emerge.

2 The Kangaroo Meets its New Neighbours

It has been said that when a polar bear meets a human being there is only one possible outcome: one of them must die. Much the same might be said of the earliest encounters between kangaroos and Europeans, except that the dying was all on the kangaroo side. The early explorers of Australia tended to shoot kangaroos for two reasons: first, they were curious about them and wanted to examine them more closely; second, they were always at the end of a long voyage on which the fresh meat had long been expended and they wanted something different to eat. Hunting kangaroos for sport or for their fur and leather came a little later. But only a little later.

If the first encounters between Europeans and kangaroos were all one-sided, it would appear that the first encounters between Indigenous Australians and kangaroos were rather more complex affairs. It is true that the first Australians hunted and killed kangaroos for food, as they still do. However, kangaroos also entered into the rich and complex symbolic world of early Australia. Kangaroos played their role in the interplay of totem and taboo, in the description of kinship relations and in the explanatory system known as the Dreaming or Dreamtime (a story that explains the creation of life, people and animals, a system still used today), in which Indigenous people inhabit a highly spiritualized

The brush-tailed rock wallaby (*Petrogale penicillata*), from John Gould, *The Mammals of Australia* (1863).

landscape full of interconnections and in which the distinction between human and animal is not solid. Kangaroo hunting, for example, is a Dreamtime experience played out in the landscape of the ancestors, an activity that renews the connection between those ancestors and the country they have shaped.

It must be remembered that Indigenous Australian culture is highly diversified (consider the list of peoples from just the Sydney Cove area given in the previous chapter) and so we cannot really speak of a single Indigenous attitude to kangaroos. We can, however, make some very broad generalizations so that the role of the kangaroo in Indigenous life can be a little better understood.

Broadly speaking, the first Australians were hunter-gatherers. The men were the hunters and the women were the gatherers. This division has made itself felt in the various artefacts that form the archaeological record and the continued craft tradition today. Boomerangs, woomeras and fire sticks are made by the men and a range of delicately woven and beautifully coloured baskets are made by the women. In addition, we find complex

An Indigenous Australian's kangaroo-skin water carrier, photographed in 1947.

and effective woven structures designed to trap fish and eels. This division of labour and cultural production along gender lines and the gendered ritual and symbolic meanings associated with the activities mean that attitudes to kangaroos are similarly gender-specific and that men and women have their own kangaroo stories and their own rituals relating to kangaroo spirits. It is not, however, possible or respectful for me to speak too much of these things. A strong feature of Australian Indigenous life – and one that appears to transcend its enormous geographic, cultural and linguistic diversity – is that many stories are secret and are to be told only to those who are in the groups for whom such knowledge is appropriate. To break this rule is akin to serious blasphemy in the European tradition and, in pre-colonial times, was punishable by death in certain circumstances. In developing this section of the book I have sought the advice of Indigenous people and am hopeful that this account is an accurate and duly respectful description of this important part of their culture which they have been generous in sharing with me.

One influential Indigenous elder with whom I have spoken about this takes the view that the appropriation and discussion of Indigenous Australian culture in settler society is simply another form of dispossession to be peacefully resisted. Openness to being taught by Indigenous people is a different matter. So, in addition to the totemic rules that apply to channelling knowledge within Indigenous society, there is also a political dimension about the rights of Indigenous Australians to cultural exclusivity.[1]

The potential secrecy of story materials means that in the astonishing flourishing of Indigenous Australian art since the early 1970s the artists, many of whom were and are elderly and significant custodians of Dreamtime stories, have always faced a tension between what they put in their paintings and what they leave out, between what they say about what their paintings represent and what they keep hidden. Some appear to have met this compromise by painting only partial versions of the full Dreamtime story they are depicting. Others have painted the full story but have developed an 'outer meaning' to share when speaking of its interpretation; they thus leave the 'inner meaning' unspoken and available only to those to whom the knowledge is proper.

The kangaroo commonly features in the rock art that forms the most tangible part of traditional Indigenous Australian culture and which has been produced from the first settlement some 50,000 years ago up to the present day. Some sites are deeply related to sacred ritual and are not for viewing; others have had to be closed off or made available with only limited access because of environmental degradation or vandalism.[2] The art is found in three main periods and, within those periods, eleven main styles have been identified.

The first period is the Pre-Estuarine, which dates between 50,000 and 8,000 years ago. We see, about 20,000 years ago, the beginnings of large outline drawings of animals including kangaroos which are then filled in various ways, sometimes with patterns, at other times with flat colours. Sometimes the animals are depicted bigger than life-size. In the Estuarine period (8,000 to 1,500 years ago) one finds a continuation of naturalistic animal drawings but by the end of the period the 'X-ray' style begins to appear and animals including kangaroos are shown with their internal organs displayed as if by an X-ray. This remains a feature in modern Tiwi art. In the Freshwater period, which dates from about 500 CE to almost the present day, the 'X-ray' style develops. Instead of being a literal rendition of bodily organs, the internal structures of the animals are modified into decorative patterns and blocks. Although rock art shows a variety of images of kangaroos, only one known site, Bare Hill in North Queensland, shows kangaroos with open mouths. The reason for this variation is unknown.

Rock art is found all over Australia but the most important concentrations are in the northern half of the continent at Kakadu and in the Kimberleys. At Wanna Munna in the Pilbara area of Western Australia there is a significant site of petroglyphs (images formed by carving rather than painting) and these include several impressive representations of kangaroos. The area around Sydney has a surprisingly rich store of rock art and the variety of what remains is a poignant reminder of what has been lost due to early urban development which made no attempt to preserve Indigenous culture. Sydney rock art includes painting, petroglyphs and engravings on the ground. Kangaroos figure commonly as do images of kangaroo tracks – the making in the sand of pictures of animal tracks was a feature of Indigenous ritual which has found its way into contemporary Indigenous painting. We can adduce some ritual relations in the rock art but in addition it is probably fair to assume that

Rock painting of a wallaby.

Indigenous Australians were also interested in using their creative talents to record what they saw, and in this record, information about the early history of Australia is often to be found that would otherwise have been lost. Rock art at Mungo National Park, for example, records megafaunal kangaroos, including what is probably the fanged kangaroo and the giant short-faced kangaroo with which the Barkindji people have a special relationship through their own Dreaming.

Kangaroos are large, powerful animals and therefore often carry very important Dreamings. Among some of the peoples of what is now called Western Australia, for example, the red kangaroo is a very significant animal indeed, but the stories associated with red kangaroos there are very deeply hidden. This may be because they are associated with sexual material and this is very often part of the most intimate levels of Indigenous knowledge.

Certainly in the early 1970s when the first generation of artists started to work in the studios of teacher Geoffrey Bardon at Papunya (near Alice Springs and the place where the modern tradition of desert painting really started; this stimulated a similar flourishing of Indigenous creativity around Australia and in the Tiwi and Torres Straits Islands), the depiction of kangaroo Dreaming was one of the most difficult areas for painters. It seems

Johnny Yukumirr, *Garrtjambal*, 1992, natural pigments on board.

to have required them to think very deeply indeed about how they might properly record kangaroo stories within a framework that was appropriately reflective of traditional culture.[3] At the time, some Indigenous people were deeply critical of the first generation of painters saying that they had revealed too much of cultural significance. In Australia today Indigenous paintings adorn every corporate boardroom and galleries selling high-quality work are to be found in every major town, but there is also the memory of the atmosphere of depression and grief which is reported to have hung over Papunya after the first day of painting.

In Tiwi art, kangaroos that are for hunting are painted (as are all hunted animals) as X-ray figures, so the vital organs are all visible beneath the fur, while kangaroos depicted as part of other stories are depicted more naturalistically, as opaque. Notice that the 'real' animals are the least realistically depicted from the Western point of view.

A recent painting by Graham King of the Pilaarkiyalu clan of the Wiradjuri and Ngiyampaa people of New South Wales – who has the grey kangaroo as his totem – is a portrait of a small black kangaroo called Enora. An analysis of the painting offers the opportunity to show how Indigenous knowledge works in the context of art presented to a non-Indigenous viewer. The kangaroo lived in the famous Aboriginal Tent Embassy in Canberra. The painting is, however, not merely a portrait of Enora. It is also a depiction of a persona of King's grandfather, and this image is associated with various objects including boomerangs, throwing sticks and a spear with a deliberately unexplained kinship design. The painting is made with ochre taken from the garden of the house at Thirroul where D. H. Lawrence lived while he was writing the novel *Kangaroo*, so the image also references the colonial history of Australia and its material form reclaims the

Graham King,
Enora, 2009,
ochre on canvas.

Indigenous heritage from that history. King's painting offers
a multi-layered image that provides a readily understandable
account of the kangaroo in Indigenous culture. It is a portrait of
a specific kangaroo but it is also a depiction of a spiritual form
within a specific kinship system, not all of which can be disclosed.
King himself describes the painting as 'for magic and healing'.

But what we see in King's painting is far more than a simply
layered interplay of the real and the symbolic. The various layers
of meaning within the work are not discreet so the painting cannot be read as either a portrait of a kangaroo or a depiction of
a spiritual form of King's grandfather. It is both simultaneously.
And neither way of seeing the painting demands that we give

primacy or priority to one interpretation over the other. In addition, there is another layer of meaning in the work that is not disclosed to viewers who are not part of the group that owns the knowledge required to unlock that meaning. The Dreaming story of the kangaroo and the kinship relationships here depicted are not to be read as symbols as we might read symbols or allegory in Western art. Instead, we are dealing with different orders of reality and the kangaroo exists in each of these orders (at least three in this painting and possibly more) not as a multiple entity but as a single being in different simultaneous dimensions. So when we speak of the Indigenous relationship with the kangaroo we speak not of a single relationship with real kangaroos or of a religious relationship with kangaroo totems or symbols, but of both at the same time. This needs to be remembered whenever we encounter Indigenous depictions of any animal or natural environment and I think it is safe to generalize this viewpoint across the whole of Indigenous Australian and Torres Strait Islands culture.

Kado Muir of the Ngalia Heritage Research Council has pointed out that the construction of the zoological category 'marsupial' is a response to the novelty of these animals in a European context and that Indigenous Australian taxonomy does not treat them as a specific category in the same way. This is because Indigenous knowledge operates in a holistic fashion in which spirituality and kinship relations are as important as physiology.

For example, in addressing *marlu* (the Warlpiri word for the red kangaroo) an Indigenous person would see a highly spiritualized animal that carries a number of important and secret stories and an animal that gives itself up to people for their nourishment. This idea of sacrifice is central to the conception of *marlu* among the Indigenous people of Western Australia. But although the red kangaroo is food, it may not be eaten by anyone connected with it through totemic kinship relations. They must care for it and perform the rituals that will sustain its spiritual power. The bereaved also may not eat red kangaroo for a year after a death, but they may eat other kinds of kangaroo meat. For these reasons, and for more practical ones – to European eyes – concerning land rights and ecology, the kangaroo industry causes Indigenous Australians some anxiety. As non-Indigenous society uses the kangaroo for food and commodities it should pay more attention to Indigenous knowledge and conceptions of kangaroos.

It is generally accepted that the first non-Indigenous depiction of a member of the kangaroo family is an engraving to be found in Cornelis de Bruijn's *Travels into Muscovy, Persia and the East Indies* and that this is actually a New Guinea dusky pademelon (now *Thylogale brunii* after de Bruijn). De Bruijn's work appeared in 1711. It should be noted that he did not see this animal in the wild but in Java, where it was kept as a pet in a small zoo maintained at the country estate of Weltevreden by Cornelis Kastelein, one of the many Dutch East India Company officers based there. In de Bruijn's account the creature was tame and delightful and had been named a 'philander' (meaning 'fond of men') – because of its tameness – by its keepers. The engraving shows an alert but somewhat objectless and even forlorn little animal. It is not shown in captivity but in a vaguely depicted naturalistic landscape of what appear to be rolling hills. In depicting this background the engraver started what became, as we shall see, an important trend in the depiction of kangaroos whereby captive or dead animals are shown in landscapes which may or may not bear any relationship to the grasslands and deserts of Australia or the forests of New Guinea. The engraving shows very clearly the most distinctive feature of this new animal, its pouch. De Bruijn recorded the marvellous friendliness of this little animal and also that colonies of it were kept on the Aru Islands specifically for food and on feast days that 'Aru rabbit' was eaten in very great quantities.

However, if de Bruijn's image of the pademelon is the first attested image of a marsupial produced by a Western artist, a much more intriguing possibility opens up when we consider the title page produced by Cornelis de Jode for the 1593 Antwerp printing of *Speculum orbis terrae*. This atlas, produced when Antwerp was still part of the Spanish Netherlands, drew on, among other things, the materials derived from the fairly extensive Portuguese and Spanish voyages of discovery during which, there can be little doubt, Australia was 'discovered' (probably by the Portuguese in the mid-fifteenth century and tantalizingly hinted at in the shape of Jave la Grande, a land mass shown in the so-called Dieppe maps dating from the early sixteenth century. The true meaning and history of these maps are much disputed by academic cartographers and we should not jump to the conclusion that they really do show Australia, attractive though that

The mala, or rufous hare wallaby (*Lagorchestes hirsutus*), from Gould, *The Mammals of Australia* (1863).

FILANDER.

Matthys Pool, engraving of the philander or De Bruijn's kangaroo, illustration for Cornelis de Bruijn, *Travels into Muscovy . . .* (1711).

conclusion may be). One map shows a large southern continent below New Guinea and separated by what are almost certainly (if you believe that these are maps of Australia) the Torres Straits (named after Luis de Torres who sailed through them in 1607). But what is really fascinating is the creature that sits in the bottom right-hand corner of the frontispiece. It looks a bit like a camel or maybe a giraffe but it has what is clearly a pouch with two little camels (or maybe giraffes) happily peering out. The pouch looks a bit like a modern baby-sling, so de Jode presumably had only a description to go on, but it is definitely a pouch. This possible marsupial shares the title page with a horse, a camel and a lion. Arguably these are so placed to represent four continents (Europe, Asia, Africa and, let us speculate, Australia) as their positions relative to each other do offer a reasonable proxy for the geographical relationships of these continents (there was some knowledge of South American marsupials so the de Jode creature could possibly represent one of them without committing too much violence to the geographical scheme).[4]

This is not especially surprising. Everyone knew that Australia was there and it is only the specific deformations of the British imperial narrative of history that have caused us to forget that in 'discovering' Australia Captain Cook was, in fact, disproving the existence of the Great Southern Continent that he was sent to find. Up to this point the assumption was that there must be a great landmass in the south to balance the continents of the northern hemisphere. By mapping Australia and New Zealand and by scouring the seas at very low latitudes Cook showed that this assumption was not true – although the Russian discovery of Antarctica in 1820 demonstrated that there was something there after all.

This misrepresentation is regrettable since it detracts from what was Cook's real achievement: the astonishingly accurate mapping of the eastern Australian and New Zealand coastlines. To give some idea of the greatness of Cook's endeavours we need only note that the combined length of his three great expeditions would have taken him and his heroic crews to the moon. In the late nineteenth century the respected illustrator and former Papal Zouave George Collingridge had his reputation largely destroyed when he pointed this out (favouring a Portuguese discovery based on the Jave la Grande theory) in his book *The Discovery of Australia* (1895). Australia simply didn't want to hear this at the time.

But de Jode and de Bruijn represent false dawns, for a flurry of kangaroo representations was about to blow across Europe,

The lower-right ornament on the title page of Cornelis de Jode's *Speculum orbis terrae* (1593) is possibly a misconstrued kangaroo.

changing forever notions about geography, zoology and taxonomy, and preparing the European mind for its first encounters with genuinely new animals.

By the late eighteenth century the two ranking imperial powers were France and Britain, and they competed, particularly in North America and India, to develop colonial domination and to build global empires. One sphere of competition that is less well remembered is Australia and, in the wake of Cook, numerous French and British expeditions sailed in southern waters vying to discover suitable places to colonize the great continent previously visited by the Portuguese, Spanish and Dutch (as well, of course, as the Chinese and the Indonesian Macassans who had been fishing and working in the sea cucumber trade and interacting with the Indigenous people in Arnhem Land and more widely along the north coast for many years before the Europeans arrived). There is also a view, which has very little support except the highly circumstantial, that Hong Bao and Zhou Man, the vice-admirals of the famous Chinese explorer

Zheng He, visited Australia in the early fifteenth century and even sent back kangaroos for the imperial gardens of Beijing.

The French mainly concentrated on what is now Western Australia, on the face of it the least promising area – although now hugely rich in mineral wealth – and so did not plant settled colonies. The later dream of Terre Napoléon never fully materialized and it was left to the British to colonize Australia, first in the form of Cook who claimed the entire continent for the Crown and completed the map of Australia in his epic voyage up the coast of New South Wales and Queensland, and then in the form of the First Fleet, which brought the first population to Botany Bay and then to Sydney Cove to establish a penal colony there.[5]

This exploration and settlement activity was accompanied by a great scientific entourage and, of course, one object of curiosity and study for this group was the kangaroo. We must remember that this was during the Enlightenment and so both French and British scientific pioneers were concerned to understand the working of the natural world without recourse to supernatural or religious frameworks. They wanted to strip the objects of their study down to an empirical analysis untrammelled by traditional forms of understanding based on authorities such as Aristotle (although it is arguable that Aristotle's impulse to classify and systematize zoological science was not so very different from the same impulse as it was manifest in the Enlightenment). This was just as well, since Aristotle had very little indeed to say about kangaroos.

Science had become a gentlemanly pursuit and learned societies became fashionable places of retreat. High-class publications such as the *Gentleman's Magazine* carried scientific articles and important engravings of new plants and animals. In today's parlance, science was the new rock 'n' roll. In addition, the European courts and some wealthy individuals had started to build

up significant collections of exotic animals based on a far more scientific classification and better discipline around display and care than was the case for the old medieval and Renaissance menageries. It is true, of course, that one motivation for all this was not pure scientific disinterestedness but the desire to use the natural world as a vehicle for displaying the superiority of the newly constructed model of the intellectual and sensible man and as a proxy for the imperial domination of colonized people.

The broad-faced potoroo (formerly the broad-faced rat-kangaroo, (*Potorous platyops*, ex *Hypsiprymnus platyops*), from Gould, *The Mammals of Australia* (1863).

As was noted in the previous chapter, the British first met the kangaroo properly on Cook's voyage up the Queensland coast. On board were the scientists Joseph Banks and Daniel Carl Solander and a band of hand-picked artists and scientists, three of whom – Sydney Parkinson, Alexander Buchan and Herman Spöring – were to die during the expedition. Banks was to become, partly as a result of his experience with Cook, the foremost naturalist of his day and it is often forgotten that to get his passage on the *Endeavour* he had to pay his own way using his spectacular private fortune to open first doors and then gangways. Banks described the first sighting of the kangaroo on 22 June 1770:

> The People who were sent to the other side of the water in order to shoot Pigeons saw an animal as large as a greyhound, of a mouse colour and very swift . . .

Three days later Banks got a better look:

> In gathering plants today I myself had the good fortune to see the beast so much talked of, tho but imperfectly; he was not only like a greyhound in size and running but had a long tail, as long as any grey hounds; what to liken him to I could not tell, nothing certainly that I have seen resembles him.

On 7 July Banks stumbled on some kangaroos and set his greyhound (he was obviously keen on greyhounds) to chase them:

> We walked many miles over the flats and saw 4 of the animals, 2 of which my greyhound fairly chas'd, but they beat him owing to the length and thickness of the grass which prevented him from running while at every bound they leaped over the tops of it. We observed much to our surprise that instead of going upon all fours this animal went upon two legs, making vast bounds just as the Jerbua (*Mus jaculus*) does.

By 14 July the story reached its sad and inevitable ending:

Our second lieutenant who was out shooting today had the good fortune to kill the animal that had so long been the subject of our speculations. To compare it to any European animal would be impossible as it has not the least resemblance of any I have seen. Its fore legs are extremely short and of no use to it in walking [this is not actually true – kangaroos often walk on their forelegs], its hind again as disproportionately long; with these it hops 7 or 8 feet at each hop in the same manner as the Gerbua, to which animal indeed it bears much resemblance except in size, this being in weight 38 lb and the Gerbua no larger than a common rat.

The next day Cook himself recorded that they ate the specimen and it provided 'most excellent meat'. By 27 July kangaroos were less novel and Banks tells us that:

This day was devoted to hunting the wild animal [the kangaroo]. We saw several and had the good fortune to kill a very large one which weighd 84 lb.

In these few journal entries we have a miniature narrative of the colonization of Australia, and indeed, a narrative of all colonization especially as it affected local animals. The second lieutenant referred to was the Virginian John Gore so we have a triumvirate – Banks, Gore and Cook – who offer a continuity of narrative action and deploy a range of European discourses: of science, of hunting and of cooking. We have the fatal confrontation of the Old and New Worlds in the form of Banks's greyhound and the solitary kangaroo (which Banks is forced to liken to a greyhound because he had no other word for it – this is, in itself, a colonizing gesture). This little Antipodean tragedy,

George Stubbs, *Kangaroo*, 1772, oil on canvas.

unfolding over three weeks, contains in itself the microcosm of the settlement of Australia and a Sibylline prophecy for the kangaroos of the future. Gore was probably not the first Englishman to shoot a kangaroo (this dubious honour almost certainly goes to an unknown crewman of Dampier's 1699 voyage down the coast of Western Australia), but his action, embedded as it is in a narrative that has its own momentum and which, in some senses, is still continuing today, has the same significance for the Indigenous people and the animals of Australia as the 'shot heard round the world' fired at Concord, Massachusetts, in 1775

John Hassall, *The Discovery of the Kangaroo*, 1904, print.

has for the shape of modern geopolitics. As well as being known for being the first Englishman (Americans were still British at this time) to have shot a kangaroo, Gore also has the unfortunate distinction of being the first to shoot a Maori.

Notice how two things happen even this early in the history of the British relationship with kangaroos. First, Banks sets his greyhounds to hunt one down. Second, the kangaroo is killed and eaten. This pattern of description, killing and eating is one we encounter time and time again as Europeans meet exotic animals and the kangaroo is not exempt. These events in the early history of European Australia caught the imagination of the first visual commentators and so we can see how central it is to our understanding of what Australia meant in colonial times and how the kangaroo featured. The incident of Banks and his greyhounds featured in a painting of 1796 by Sydenham Teak Edwards, best known as a botanical illustrator. This image was used as the basis of an engraving for the catalogue *Museum Leverianum*, a depiction of the wonders on show in Sir Ashton Lever's museum at Leicester Square. The currently lost 1889 painting of *Captain Cook Taking Possession of the Australian Continent on Behalf of the British Crown* shows Cook making his claim while to one side two men skin a kangaroo and a dog (Banks's greyhound, one assumes) looks on.[6]

Also on board the *Endeavour* was the artist Sydney Parkinson who made a number of sketches of kangaroos – perhaps the first attestable European images of kangaroos proper. They are merely sketches but they convey a good sense of the kangaroo both still and in motion. Although Parkinson himself died with a number of Cook's crew during a fever-ridden stop in Batavia on the voyage home, his sketches were sufficient (once Banks had got legal control of them from Parkinson's brother) to furnish the much more celebrated artist George Stubbs, already known as a specialist in animal paintings, with material for the first full-scale painting of a kangaroo. This was done to Banks's commission and sourced from a combination of Parkinson's sketches and the skull and inflated skin of a kangaroo brought home by Banks and given to the famous surgeon John Hunter for study. The painting was completed by 1773. The skull survived until the Second World War when it was destroyed in a bombing raid that damaged the Hunterian Museum in London. It does, however, apparently live on in a photograph, which I have unfortunately not been able to locate.[7]

Stubbs's painting shows what is probably an eastern grey kangaroo. It is alert, with erect ears and is turning its head. This is a characteristic gesture of kangaroos so it is clearly traceable to a possible posture taken by the kangaroo when it was being sketched, but I also wonder if the animal is turning to notice the approach of Banks's greyhound and reacting to the report of a musket and the distant puff of smoke which might be fascinating it in that brief moment before the lead ball arrives and it crumples to the earth. I have made the point elsewhere that during the Enlightenment, landscape often seems to have been viewed down the barrel of a fowling piece and here we see a kangaroo just at the point of its own extermination. The animal is set in an interesting and somewhat picturesque landscape with a mountain in the background and suitably spaced trees beneath a highly conventionalized cloudscape. There is nothing specifically Australian about this setting and this, I think, makes the kangaroo a more exotic creature since the viewer, by being presented with only the clichés of the European picturesque tradition, is not distracted from the main subject matter. Notice that the kangaroo is male, one assumes, for its pouch is not prominently displayed, as I suspect it would be if it had been female. At the beginning of the twentieth century the British artist John Hassall published a woodcut of the discovery of the kangaroo which shows two eighteenth-century seamen, one prostrate in amazement, looking at a group of kangaroos, one of which looks back in an attitude that owes much to the Stubbs painting.

Stubbs's painting became the benchmark or archetype for English depictions of kangaroos for many years after. A version of it was engraved as the frontispiece of Bankes's *New System of Geography* (*c.* 1788) but here the landscape has been substantially altered. The kangaroo no longer stands on what appears to be an isolated rocky outcrop; the rocks are still there but now they are surrounded by trees. The background trees in Stubbs's painting have been pulled forward and the background mountain has been reduced in scale. This is a kangaroo displayed not as a zoological specimen as Stubbs designed, but as a creature naturalized within an English parkland. As we will see, this is not a far-fetched notion. I have seen a photograph of a stuffed kangaroo being removed from an Australian natural history museum. The image is not dated but looks as though it may have been taken in the 1920s or earlier. The kangaroo has been mounted in the posture of the kangaroo in Stubbs's painting, which shows very well not only how powerful Stubbs's image was in determining what a kangaroo should look like but also how dominant this English construction of an Australian animal proved to be.

In the version of the Stubbs painting engraved as an accompaniment to the first edition of Cook's *Endeavour* journals in 1773, the image is reversed and the kangaroo looks from right to left. The background has again been changed: the hills are more rolling and the reed-like plants adjacent to the kangaroo in Stubbs's picture have been very clearly realized as some sort of exotic plant. This is the kangaroo in its natural setting, transporting the reader of Cook's journals to a far-off land of strange animals and new plants.

These three main versions of the Stubbs image (including the archetype) were followed by many more. Most notable among these is perhaps the woodcut in Thomas Bewick's hugely influential *A General History of Quadrupeds*, which went through six editions between 1791 and 1823. The kangaroo appeared in the first edition and was subsequently reproduced unchanged (the

wombat – or wombach – did not make an appearance until the fifth edition in 1807). It stands isolated on the page with only a hint of a natural environment and is solely designed to show the reader what a kangaroo looks like.

Bewick's charming woodcut contrasts with the somewhat more formal renditions in Thomas Pennant's *History of the Quadrupeds* in which Stubbs's kangaroo stands in isolation on a much smaller rock. The first edition of Pennant's book came out in 1781; in the 1793 edition the basic form is the same and the animal still stands alone on a rock without further natural context, although advances in kangaroo studies had led the engraver to

'An animal found on the coast of New Holland called kanguroo', 1773, engraving after the painting by George Stubbs.

Thomas Thornton, 'An animal found on the coast of New Holland called kanguroo', illustration after the painting by George Stubbs; from John Hawkesworth, *Account of the voyages undertaken by the order of His present Majesty for making discoveries in the southern hemisphere . . .* (1773).

WONDERFUL MUSEUM.

Thornton sculp

An Animal found on the Coast *of* NEW HOLLAND, called KANGUROO.

make substantial alterations to the figure of the kangaroo: its face is leaner and its feet are very much better realized. These changes may have been the result of two exhibitions. In 1789 a kangaroo skeleton and skin were exhibited in London which, as Ronald Younger has pointed out, challenged in their bulk and obvious hardiness the familiar received image of the animal. Then in 1791 a live kangaroo was exhibited; this will be dealt with in detail in the next chapter. A version of the Stubbs image also appeared as an engraving in the *Gentleman's Magazine* at this time.

In George Shaw's *General Zoology; or, Systematic Natural History* of 1800, a cluster of kangaroos – one of which is apparently flying – is clearly based on a Parkinson sketch and surrounds the Stubbsian figure, but here the feet have been enhanced and the ears reduced to create a somewhat fierce-looking animal with a hint of nasty teeth and vicious claws. The landscape acts as neither ornament nor distraction but simply as a functional backdrop. This is the kangaroo as imperial conquest, the wild animal domiciled through the enlightened understanding of the European scientist.

These first, fleeting glimpses of the kangaroo made by explorers were soon replaced by the more sustained contact with the creatures experienced by the gentleman, sailors, soldiers and convicts brought to settle Australia in January 1788 by the First Fleet (the eleven ships which brought 1,487 people, 778 of whom were convicts). Of the free travellers, several had artistic abilities or, being officers, had been trained in drawing for military purposes and now turned their hand to recording the local curiosities that would soon be part of their everyday lives. Images varied in quality and accuracy between the strong but naive images done by the officers John Hunter and William Bradley and the somewhat more polished but effete renditions done by

Vignette of a kangaroo by Thomas Bewick, c. 1790.

Kang-oo-roo — or Pa-ta-ga-rang

140 th Weight

John Hunter, watercolour sketch of an eastern grey kangaroo, c. 1788–90.

Sarah Stone (who was based in London and, presumably, did the illustrations from sketches) for John White, the First Fleet's surgeon. Stone's image is an interesting one since it varies very considerably from the Stubbsian archetype discussed above but maintains the convention of setting a kangaroo on a rock. Stone's picture concentrates on the two most startling things about the kangaroo's body: its pouch (which is shown much as de Bruijn

depicted the pademelon's pouch) and the great disparity in scale between its massively muscled hind legs and residual forearms, which, in Stone's drawing, hang almost lifelessly.

A drawing done by surgeon Arthur Bowes Smith is especially interesting because it is essentially a copy of one of the engravings of Stubbs's kangaroo, probably the one from the first edition of Cook's *Endeavour* journals which would have been required reading for all First Fleet officers. The artist lived among kangaroos and yet he chose to copy the well-established English model. This was, of course, probably because drawing a live kangaroo is not easy and Smith was not a trained artist. But drawing landscape is not so difficult and the image does not suggest that Bowes Smith was concerned to produce anything like a realistic depiction of the Australian landscape. So here the kangaroo has already been transformed into an artefact of colonization and a superior European version in the form of the Stubbs archetype has been imported into Australia. The kangaroo has, thus, already become naturalized as part of an English culture and, as we will see, this process continued throughout much of the nineteenth century.

Perhaps the most charming of the First Fleet kangaroo drawings is that by the midshipman George Raper, better known now for his botanical illustrations. Raper's kangaroo is not an especially good likeness (Stubbs did better from a skull and an inflated skin), but it has a remarkable presence that seems to emanate from the combination of the naivety of Raper's technique and his apparent disbelief that such an animal could really exist. The kangaroo's forearms are, as in Sarah Stone's paintings, attenuated to an exaggerated degree. But what is really interesting in Raper's image is the fact that the kangaroo is set in a distinctively Australian landscape. Or is it? It stands beside an exotic reed-like plant. But this plant, although naturalistically drawn in Raper's image and a testament to his skill as a botanical illustrator, is precisely the same as those less well delineated in the version of the Stubbs painting engraved as the frontispiece to Cook's *Endeavour* journals. So although Raper is producing a distinctively Australian picture, his compositional technique and the detail with which he furnishes his picture refers the reader back to the 'Bible' of Australian settlement, Cook's journals and, once again, effectively imports the kangaroo into Australia. I do not think it has been previously observed that kangaroos arrived in Australia with the First Fleet, but the ways in which the First Fleet artists approached their depiction strongly suggests that this was the case.

So far we have looked at the kangaroo only as it was constructed by the First Fleet's free artists. When we turn to the convicts we find that the approach was slightly different. By no means all the convict artists left pictures of kangaroos – the artists known as the Port Jackson Painter and the Sydney Cove Painter

George Raper,
*Gum-plant, &
Kangooroo of
New-Holland*,
c. 1789, drawing.

did not – but two, Thomas Watling and Richard Browne, did. Watling was a forger and therefore an accomplished draughtsman. While his painting is not technically of a kangaroo but of swamp wallaby, it is a lively affair showing the animal poised in the midst of hopping on the balls of its strong feet. Watling's

Joseph Lycett,
Aborigines Hunting Kangaroos,
c. 1815–20,
watercolour.

concentration on this moment is the first really strong depiction of the other distinctive feature of the kangaroo, its locomotion. Richard Browne's kangaroo is a wonderfully naive four-square creature looking somewhat like a country gentleman surveying his estate. But neither Browne nor Watling appears to have been influenced by Stubbs. This might be because as convicts they did not have access to the relevant engraving, but this is only speculation. Browne was working to produce pictures for the journal of William Skottowe, the governor of the penal colony at Newcastle, and so would presumably have been furnished with some materials to contextualize his work. My sense is that the originality of the Browne and Watling images has more to do with their status as convicts. Unlike the free settlers they had no hope of ever getting back home (although theoretically they could buy a passage once they had served their term – in Watling's case fourteen years) and so there was no psychological impetus to import that home into Australia. I would claim that, imperfect as they are, what we see in the works of the convict artists are the first genuine, non-Indigenous Australian depictions of the kangaroo. In addition, the minimal backgrounds to the convict painting perhaps show their own attitude to their new country: it is absent of meaning and is only a place to stand.

By 1819, when the colony was well established, the professional artist John Lewin was still producing kangaroo images that, if not directly influenced by Stubbs, were still contextualized by a pastoralizing impulse out of the European tradition of picturesque landscape. We see the same thing in the painted panels of two important items of early colonial furniture, the Macquarie chest and the Dixson chest. These were made to contain collections of natural history specimens and were decorated with various paintings of the Australian landscape, including one panel in each (the chests are clearly related to each other) showing two kangaroos. These were probably produced by the convict artist Joseph Lycett partly as modified copies of the engravings (done by John Byrne and based on William Westall's painting) found as illustrations in Matthew Flinders's *A Voyage to Terra Australis*. Some of Lycett's pictures were themselves subsequently engraved as illustrations in James Wallis's *Australian Views*. Lycett does not show the influence of Stubbs but nor does he achieve a distinctively Australian vision, and in this he differs from other convict artists. The reason for this is probably related to the specific patronage networks within that he found himself. He was working for prestigious and powerful men and producing objects of the highest quality and rarity. It was therefore incumbent on him to produce kangaroos that conformed to the English model and the English taste, and that is what he did.[8]

While the colony was being developed at Sydney, other major British expeditions were under way; these were the marathon explorations carried out by Matthew Flinders between 1798 and 1803. These included a circumnavigation of the continent, and the first voyage was informed by the lively observations of the scientist George Bass (who recorded a notable encounter with a wombat on the Furneaux Islands in his journal). The Flinders expeditions were crucial to the opening up of Australia but various catastrophes meant that their importance was, perhaps, less well recognized than Cook's various voyages and the artwork they generated was not disseminated nearly as well as that produced as a result of Cook's activities. This was partly because Flinders's landscape artist William Westall was less than diligent – in spite of having the direct patronage of Banks – and partly because of a new outbreak of the Napoleonic wars, which would go on with only a short respite until 1815; this meant that the wonderful work of Ferdinand Bauer, Flinders's other artist, was not published until the late 1990s.

Bauer's illustrations were of the highest quality and would certainly have pre-empted the luxury market subsequently occupied by John Gould. Bauer produced the first real attempts to depict accurate zoology within a high-end production, and his work should have introduced a whole new concept of the kangaroo in both Britain and Australia: a kangaroo that looked like a kangaroo and which was not hampered by the Stubbsian orthodoxy. But because of the much-delayed publication of Bauer's works it was not really until the mid-nineteenth century and the publication of the three volumes of John Gould's *The Mammals of Australia* between 1845 and 1863 (one volume was exclusively devoted to macropods) that the British public saw the kinds of zoological illustration that made it possible for them to see the kangaroo as more than a natural curiosity, more than a symbol of a new country and as a thing in itself depicted in loving detail.[9]

However, if the British public had to wait so long, the French public had access to high-quality images rather earlier. French attempts to compete with Britain to colonize Australia did not

The ursine (formerly black) tree-kangaroo (*Dendrolagus ursinus*), from Gould, *The Mammals of Australia* (1863).

succeed (the ill-fated Jean-François de la Perouse reached Botany Bay just a single day after the First Fleet, and Bruni d'Entrecasteaux had his ships confiscated by the Dutch), but that did not prevent a very serious effort in scientific exploration headed by Captain Nicolas Baudin, who is much less well known in France than Cook is in Britain. Baudin's main achievement was probably bringing thousands (sources vary between 100,000 and 200,000) of specimens back to Europe. But the artwork from his voyage (1800–03) offers a very different image of the kangaroo from the British depictions and, indeed, an entirely different style of representation. The Stubbs image was, of course, not unknown in France and was used to illustrate editions of Buffon's *Histoire naturelle* (1779–88) and other books elsewhere in Europe and in the United States, but by the time Baudin's artist Charles-Alexandre Lesueur arrived on the scene the new French revolutionary government had already put the principles of the Enlightenment into practice and its successor, Napoleon, was seeking a new way of showing the kangaroo.[10]

Lesueur obliged and his illustrations show an extraordinary delicacy. The kangaroo and the other inhabitants of Terre Napoléon exist in a world of pastoral innocence quite different from the European Picturesque described above with regard to the English painters. For the French, the kangaroo becomes not an artefact of colonization but a fresh and free inhabitant of a new world sufficiently uncorrupted to carry a projection of Rousseauesque idealism. The magnificent record of the Baudin expedition was published in 1807 and represented an entirely new way of seeing Australia and the kangaroo. This French depiction is a far more Romantic image than anything that British artists produced and shows how the kangaroo was capable of bearing a different set of cultural values when its image was contextualized by the revolutionary approach to the natural world espoused in France. But although Napoleon was not happy with Baudin (who died en route back to France before Napoleon could carry out his threat to hang him), he was pleased with his finds and the Empress Joséphine set up an Australian garden and menagerie at Malmaison. It is worth noting that the frontispiece to *Voyage de découvertes aux terres Australes* by Lesueur and his colleague Nicolas Martin Petit shows the Australian garden complete with three kangaroos and some emus on the lawns and black swans on the lake.

However, kangaroos had been seen in France before the return of the Baudin expedition and the establishment of the Australian garden at Malmaison. In 1789 Joseph Banks had sent a live kangaroo to his friend Pierre Broussonet, who had been helping him in the matter of building a British-based flock of merino sheep (Australia built its first fortune on these animals, a pound of whose wool will produce 92 miles of yarn). Unfortunately, this kangaroo arrived only a few days before the storming of the Bastille and sinks from history – the Duke of Devonshire, who had arranged a cricket tour of France for the same fateful month, had the good sense to cancel – and it is unclear what befell it. If it went to the royal menagerie nothing good would have happened, since although the revolution's ideologists made common cause with the king's animals and saw them as fellow victims of the monarchic regime's tyranny, the creatures were, in fact, slaughtered by the mob. French zoos are unlucky places: the animals in the Jardin des Plantes during the Prussian siege of 1870–71 were sold off at high prices to keep the rich from starving and we know that at least one kangaroo suffered that fate.

In 1802, during the Peace of Amiens – a lull in the long European wars stimulated by the French Revolution – a brief and productive dialogue took place between French and British scientists who had been out of touch for a decade. Banks sent his French counterpart Georges Cuvier a platypus and was advised by his friend Sir Charles Blagden that the young Napoleon, who at that time styled himself First Consul, might like a kangaroo or two:

It has occurred to me . . . that perhaps the most acceptable present that could be made to the First Consul, would

be a pair of live Kangaroos . . . The Park of St Cloud, where
he is going to reside, would be an excellent place for a little
paddock of Kangaroos, like that of the King at Richmond.

But even in this period of Anglo-French rapprochement Banks
did not like the look of Napoleon and certainly was not going to
waste any of his precious kangaroos on pleasing a dictator. A
couple of weeks later Blagden wrote again:

As to the Kangaroos, it is entirely my suggestion and let
it take its fate. Had I the honour of advising his Majesty,
my counsel would be, to send a pair of them, as a present
to the First Consul, without delay, and I should give this
advice, not from a blind admiration of the man (for I am
as sharp sighted in discerning faults as my neighbor) but
from the conviction, that more is often gained by trifling
personal civilities, than by great sacrifices.

Banks wasn't impressed by that either, or by Blagden's suggestion that Napoleon be made a Fellow of the Royal Society, over
which Banks held almost despotic sway by this time of his life.
But Napoleon didn't need English kangaroos anyway: he could
get his own from the late Captain Baudin. And he did.[11]

It was also a French writer who produced the first story that
depicted an Australian setting, complete with kangaroos. This
was *Antony; ou, La conscience* by Madame de Renneville (Sophie
de Senneterre) and it appeared in 1812 or 1813. In this moral tale,
the boy Antony is shipwrecked and enjoys various adventures,
which include a spell under the tutelage of Omaï who, in spite of
his Tahitian name, is actually an Indigenous Australian. Among
other things, Antony is shown how to hunt kangaroo (which in
this fictive world live in hollow trees).

The banded hare-wallaby (*Lagostrophus fasciatus*, ex *Lagorchestes fasciatus*), from Gould, *The Mammals of Australia* (1863).

In 1836 Ernest Fouinet's *Allan, le jeune déporté à Botany Bay* was one of a large number of French novels with an Australian setting and is notable for a scene in which a female kangaroo removes her joey from her pouch to see if it is injured and, in a notable display of sensibility, kisses it before replacing it. In 1810 the French traveller Thomas Smith published *Le Cabinet du jeune naturaliste; ou, Tableaux interéssants de l'histoire des animaux*. This includes an engraving of a man fighting a boxing kangaroo – while a caged monkey watches with interest – which apparently records a scene that Smith had witnessed on a visit to the Exeter 'Change menagerie in 1806.

French readers, especially French children, seem thus to have had more contact with kangaroos in the earliest days of European contact but, as we shall see in the following chapters, their British counterparts soon had the chance to catch up.

3 The Kangaroo at Home

Skippy, Skippy, Skippy the bush kangaroo,
Skippy, Skippy, Skippy our friend ever true.

These words and the kangaroo-hopping music that goes with them must be familiar to everyone in the Western world who is, at the time of writing, over 50 years of age. *Skippy*, the popular TV series which ran in Australia between 1966 and 1968, was syndicated well into the 1970s, so will also be known by many others in the vast array of countries in which this was the case. Various remakes and low-budget films in the succeeding years have maintained its recognizability.

For Australians *Skippy* has a particular resonance and was particularly influential. In 1966 mass television was still relatively new in Australia – it was introduced in 1956 and then only in Sydney – and programming depended heavily (as it still tends to) on material bought in from the UK, Europe and the US. *Skippy* offered Australians, for almost the first time, stories which reflected Australian interests and, more importantly, the series's bush setting showed the Australian audience just how magnificent their country was. It also inculcated the kind of national pride that was needed at a time when anxieties over the UK's dalliance with the Common Market and the grave threat that that posed to the Australian economy were in the air and when widespread despair and civil conflict over the Australian deployment in Vietnam were depressing the public mood.

Rangers Matt Hammond and Jerry King look on as Skippy goes to the rescue again, c. 1967.

Skippy tells the adventures of Sonny Hammond, a park ranger's youngest son (who lives in an almost entirely male world where women – 'girls' as they are called – are another species, treated much as they are in the British public school stories of the 1930s), and his friend Skippy, a preternaturally gifted eastern grey kangaroo. Skippy is female and so she plays a role not unlike that of the motherly Kanga, the only female in the all-male world of the Hundred Acre Wood in A. A. Milne's Winnie the Pooh books. Although the tongues of the programme makers were at times firmly in their cheeks (kangaroos don't generally play drums and they certainly don't communicate with humans through a series of intelligible clicks), the plots of the various programmes did address central Australian concerns – the management of the bush environment, for example – as well as inviting the audience to think about some of its prejudices and the kind of country that Australia ought to be. Consider the episode in which Sonny and Skippy encounter a group of Indigenous Australians. Sonny's father tells him: 'These people will never hurt you', and this offers a very different view of first people from that which was, unfortunately, all too common in the Australia of the 1960s. It is also made clear that Skippy is a wild animal; she is not a pet and lives in the bush (while also being perfectly at home with soft furnishings) and this too, I think, would have appealed to the Australian audience and contrasted vividly with the 'pet' wild animals that were the stock of American programmes of a similar kind. Until 2003 an attraction called Waratah Wildlife Park operated in the area where the programmes were originally filmed and you could go and see kangaroos there – including, of course, one that was supposed to be Skippy herself.

Skippy thus offered a view of Australia in which significant meaning was carried by a small kangaroo. The animal herself was not a metaphor for Australia but, rather, provided a way of seeing Australia and Australian concerns and thus appealed not only to the home audience but also to people in dozens of other countries. However, the idea of a friendly kangaroo was not, in itself, an original one in the context of Australian children's culture and this may account for Skippy's immediate popularity.

During the colonial period there had been a number of works featuring kangaroos. In 1858, for example, Anne Bowman's *The Kangaroo Hunters; or, Adventures in the Bush* presented a tale of imperial pluck and offered the kangaroo as a fierce and aggressive creature, one of the many hazards that infested the Australian landscape and something that the children of the empire

ENCOUNTER WITH A KANGAROO NEAR BENALLA.—SEE PAGE 11.

Samuel Calvert, 'Encounter with a Kangaroo near Benalla [Victoria]', wood engraving from the *Illustrated Australian News for Home Readers* (1874).

would do well to exterminate. A very different position was adopted by Ethel Pedley in her *Dot and the Kangaroo* (1899), in which the relationship between the young heroine and a friendly marsupial forms the core of a story with a strong conservation message at its heart. In this respect, Pedley's novel is like the even more successful *Seven Little Australians* (1894) by Ethel Turner, even though in this novel kangaroos play only a bit part as a feature of the landscape. Like *Skippy*, all these early children's books had a strong message about the importance of conserving the uniquely Australian environment of the bush and the unique wildlife of Australia. In Dorothy Wall's popular Blinky

Bill series (begun in 1933) a koala is the main character, but a kangaroo called Splodge is one of Blinky's friends and, again, the books promote a strong message about conservation.[1] In the case of *Dot and the Kangaroo*, as in the case of *Skippy*, a kangaroo is used to carry the burden of this message.

There were many other books which presented Australia both to the British and to Australians themselves as they came to understand their new home and many of these included kangaroos, often in association with accounts of Indigenous life that make very uncomfortable reading today. In Mrs Campbell Praed's *Australian Life, Black and White* (1885), the writer describes her homestead in which a pet kangaroo lives in the garden and exercises itself daily by jumping over hurdles. Alexander Mac-Donald's *The Quest of the Black Opals: A Tale of Adventure in the Heart of Australia* (1908) devotes a section to kangaroos, while in George Manville Fenn's *The Dingo Boys; or, the Squatters of Wallaby Range* (1892), we find a description of a fight with a kangaroo very similar to that encountered in Anne Bowman's earlier work:

> they saw Shanter [an Indigenous Australian] in the act of hurling his spear at a gigantic kangaroo – one of the old men of which they had heard stories – and this great animal was evidently making for the black, partly enraged by a blow it had received, partly, perhaps, to cover the flight of the herd . . . The next instant the kangaroo was upon Shanter, grasping him with its forepaws . . .

Images of kangaroo hunting were becoming extremely common in illustrated papers and it was important for the animal to be presented as fierce and bad. In William Thomes's *The Gold Hunter's Adventures; or, Life in Australia* (1864), for example, there

The 'Attractions of the Zoo' in Melbourne in 1893 included kangaroos.

THE ATTRACTIONS OF THE ZOO

is a very nasty encounter with a group of Indigenous Australians which revolves around the eating of kangaroo meat.

So we can see that in Australian children's literature and in other writing from the colonial and federation periods through to the mid-twentieth century nature and especially conservation are central themes and, in some cases, kangaroos bear the weight of those themes. This also happens in *Skippy*. However, the theme of conservation and anxiety about the preservation of Australian wildlife was by no means an invention of the liberal nineteenth century or a concern of the twentieth, when the impact of European settlement on wildlife was becoming uncomfortably clear. In fact, this anxiety seems to have been imported almost as soon as the first convicts staggered ashore in 1788. In July 1837, for example, the *Colonial Times* (a newspaper published in Hobart) carried a letter in which concern was expressed over the state of the environment and attention was drawn particularly to the clear and progressive depletion of the local kangaroo population. Two weeks later another letter appeared drawing attention to the plight of the farmer in the face of the onslaught of marsupial pests and recommending a less gentle policy. This exchange could happen in almost identical terms in any Australian newspaper today and it reminds us of the duality that the kangaroo can exhibit or manifest in Australian culture. It is simultaneously a wonderful thing and a nuisance. It is a national symbol and a piece of meat on a plate. It is an icon of environmental and cultural resilience and sustainability and a fragile mammal under varying degrees of threat.

This duality was perhaps best expressed in early Australia in a poem by the wonderfully named Barron Field. Field was a judge who found himself in a colonial posting and was by no means content: 'Where's no past tense the ignorant present's all' was his grumpy verdict. However, in 1819, two years after his arrival, he published his *First Fruits of Australian Poetry*, the first book of verse to be printed in Australia. This volume included his poem 'The Kangaroo', which ends with the lines:

> Better proportion'd animal,
> More graceful or ethereal,
> Was never follow'd by the hound,
> With fifty steps to thy one bound.
> Thou can'st not be amended: no;
> Be as thou art: thou best art so,
>
> When sooty swans are once more rare,
> And duck-moles the Museum's care,
> Be still the glory of this land,
> Happiest Work of finest Hand!

In this poem Field recognizes all too clearly the unique features of the kangaroo and its zoological wonders while locating these features very specifically in the particular conditions of Australia. He sees it as an animal for hunting as well as an adornment of the Australian landscape. But it is the final stanza that shows the tension in the poem and the cracking of the image of the kangaroo into a site of simultaneous wonder and anxiety. Here the poem becomes strangely prescient of the fate of Australian wildlife with the kangaroo carrying the burden of the rupture between conservation and exploitation.

This rupture is addressed in the work of other nineteenth-century Australian poets, such as John Dunmore Lang and Charles Harpur, who also fell upon the kangaroo as they strove to explore the complexities of a largely urban and European society that was seeking to grow in an entirely alien and often supremely unfamiliar and hostile environment. Lang's 'Australian Hymn' shows how the kangaroo was fast becoming the indispensible emblem of the colonies:

The rudest mortal under Heaven,
Stern nature's long-forgotten child!
Compatriot of the tall Emu,
The Wombat and the Kangaroo!

Here the Indigenous Australian takes his place alongside the native animals (until 1967 Indigenous people were, constitutionally, counted as part of the flora and fauna and they were not included in official census data until 1971), but, to be fair to Lang, his aim is to rescue them from their perceived barbarism as the civilizing and nurturing influences of the empire come to bear.

In the later twentieth century this duality is perhaps best expressed in Ted Kotcheff's film *Wake in Fright* (1971, also known as *Outback*), which is based on a 1961 novel of the same name by Kenneth Cook. Although this production was popular in Europe and drew rave reviews in the UK and France, its uncompromising and disturbing picture of life in remote Australia (the poster read: 'Have a drink, mate? Have a fight mate? Have a taste of dust and sweat, mate? There's nothing else out here') was too uncomfortable for Australian audiences and the film became a 'lost masterpiece' of the Australian cinematic renaissance until it was rediscovered and re-released in 2009.

In the film a city-based teacher is marooned in an outback town after losing all his money in the traditional gambling game of two-up. The brutality of the town's male inhabitants – they think he is a homosexual because he talks to women (which is, arguably, the dark side of the idyllic all-male universe inhabited by Sonny Hammond in *Skippy*) – and the brutalizing effect of the extreme landscape strip away his veneer of culture and education. The shocking set piece of the film is a violent and explicit kangaroo hunt in which the protagonist slashes a wounded kangaroo to death. It is a scene that still causes controversy today for its use of footage of the actual slaughter of kangaroos. This episode is taken fairly directly from the novel where it provides a horrific depiction of the brutality of the society in which the protagonist finds himself. Both *Skippy* and *Wake in Fright* use a kangaroo (or kangaroos) to explore the fragility of the environment in the face of contemporary Australian culture. In the former case this context is idealized, in the latter case it is deeply dystopic.

The terrifying imagery of *Wake in Fright* has more recently been countered by two documentaries. In the first, *Marluku Wirlinyi: The Kangaroo Hunters* (1998), a group of elderly Warlpiri men use a kangaroo hunt to demonstrate and explain the practice of their culture. This film was directed by the Indigenous film-makers Timothy Japangardi Marshall and Craig Japangardi Williams and gives a rare and moving insight into a world that is simultaneously, it sometimes feels, both living and dying. The other counterbalance is the beautifully crafted *Kangaroos: Faces in Mob* (2007). This film was made over a two-year period by Jan Aldenhoven and Glen Carruthers during which time they lived with a mob of kangaroos. The film shows the individual personalities of creatures that are all too easy to only see en masse. The film follows the lives of two individuals – who are given names – and offers Australians a chance to see an animal with which they thought they were familiar in new and astonishingly affecting ways.

In Baz Luhrmann's epic film *Australia* (2008) the initial journey by truck across the Northern Territory is ornamented by an

Your Flag! My Flag!!

Now, in the cause of Liberty
God help us guard it well;
Guard it till death or victory,
Guard it 'gainst Earth and
Hell.

He needs just all our sympathy, that man with soul asleep,
Whose heart exulteth not nor fills with quicken'd blood, that deep
His inmost being thrills.
Who feels not in his throat the strain of surging, keen desire,
The spirit's flame that riseth from a loyal heart afire;
When, waving in the breeze, he sees his Country's Flag!—*his* Flag!
He needs just all our sympathy whose heart is not made glad.

ALEC BARR

accompaniment of bounding kangaroos which delight the aristocratic English heroine. Her delight soon turns to horror when
one is shot and its blood trickles down the windscreen in front
of her. Scenes from the film that did not make the final cut apparently show a baby red kangaroo called Ned. Here the kangaroo
is used first to place the action unambiguously in Australia. It
then features as a contradiction: it is both a source of aesthetic
pleasure for the foreigner, especially since it signifies her arrival
in a strange land, and also a source of food to be slaughtered as
and when required by the locals. In this scene Luhrmann neatly
captures the long history of contradiction and paradox which
has been the kangaroo's lot.

We can see that the kangaroo is bound to carry a very heavy
and very special burden, for although the (European and Asian)
Australian experience is and always has been overwhelmingly

'Your Flag! My Flag!!', kangaroo patriotism on an old postcard.

A brass breastplate made for 'Bulgra, King of Arremutta [New South Wales], 1920' with a kangaroo engraved at one end.

urban, the Australian imagination lives in the outback. The Australian urban middle-classes dress in the expensively marketed clothes of R. M. Williams, the self-styled bush outfitters, and they wear the equally expensive Akubra hat with its allusions both to the intrepid bushmen and to the brave diggers of Gallipoli, Fromelles, Kokoda and Tobruk (the Akubra company uses this as a key marketing tool and the names of its designs, especially the designs of its 'heritage' range, reflect the contours of a heroic version of Australian history). They motor around the freeways of Sydney delivering their children to school in mighty Japanese four-wheel drive, off-road vehicles which could cope with the most rugged of bush terrain. Australia has, in this sense, inherited from England – another country where the majority experience is overwhelmingly urban, and has been since the middle of the nineteenth century – the nostalgia for the greenwood but this is now transformed into a colonial dream of the parched yellow landscapes of the Heidelberg School of painters and the red outback scenes of Russell Drysdale. It is, therefore, no surprise that the kangaroo, master of these imagined ideal environments, stands proudly on the national coat of arms. It is an edible creature which, like its partner on the coat of arms, the emu, is incapable of taking a backward step.

The kangaroo, often with its head turned in the manner of the Stubbs painting, came to be used as a heraldic animal in Australia from the very earliest periods of European settlement. The emblems on the flags and coats of arms of states and cities often feature a kangaroo. The arms of Melbourne and Victoria are perhaps the best examples and offer the prototype for the national coat of arms. The pattern of coats of arms with kangaroos was fixed in 1901 when the official emblems of Australia were adopted at the time of federation.

The kangaroo was also frequently featured on the so-called king-plates awarded by the settlers to Indigenous people with whom they were able to deal – this habit often caused immense disruption in traditional societies since the 'kings' thus created often did not have any senior status in their own communities, creating huge difficulties for the first people's sense of correct kinship and social relationships.

There is currently a debate in Australia over the national flag. Many Australians believe that there should no longer be a Union flag as part of the design (an equal number, or more, believe exactly the opposite, which is a fairly normal political situation in Australia), but if Australia ever does become a republic it will probably look hard at a new flag and one design that has been seriously advanced includes a large gold kangaroo as the most distinctive and recognizable symbol of things Australian.

However, the kangaroo as heraldic or quasi-heraldic beast has also found itself in many other settings in which primarily European artefacts have been 'Australianized' through the use of kangaroo figurations. In the later nineteenth century we find a number of examples. The first is the Australian ware developed by the Doulton pottery company for export to a growing colonial market that was first shown in 1879 at the Sydney International Exhibition. The National Museum of Australia has a wonderful kangaroo umbrella stand which was modelled by the eccentric George Tinworth, Doulton's star craftsman and the only Doulton potter allowed to sign his name in a visible place on a pot. This umbrella stand was first exhibited as an example of the extremely high quality of the pottery at the Chicago World's Columbian Exposition (World's Fair) of 1893. Tinworth is best known for the bizarre series of pottery mice – engaged in such human activities as steeple-chasing while riding frogs or electrocuting each other in failed attempts to set up new technologies – which was much admired by the wealthy adherents of the Arts and Crafts Movement, and this kangaroo is a rare departure into large-scale modelling. The fact that an artist of Tinworth's stature was able to produce this work shows the importance and esteem in which Doulton held the Australian market. More evidence of this is to be found in a vase decorated with kangaroos by Doulton's star animal painter Hannah Barlow. This was not produced for the Sydney Exhibition and, in fact, Barlow's first use of kangaroo images date from 1878. These two ceramic items show how naturally a company in England that wished to develop good sales in Australia (as well as in England) turned to the kangaroo to bear its marketing message.[2]

The next two examples were developed in Australia itself. The first is the carved kangaroos which, together with other semi-mythical beasts, decorate the original buildings of the

clockwise from top left
A contemporary version of an anonymous entry in the 1901 Federal Flag Design Competition.

Promotional flag designed by Lunn-Dyer & Associates for Ausflag, the body promoting the adoption of a new Australian flag.

Ian Giles's entry in a flag competition conducted by *A Current Affair*, 1993.

Athol Kelly's proposed, privately promoted 'All Australian Flag' of 1979.

Athol Kelly's proposed, privately promoted 'All Australian Flag' of 1979.

John Williamson's 'True Blue' flag, 1995.

An entry in the Ausflag design competition of 1994, designed by Harold Scruby.

An entry in the Ausflag design competition of 1993, designed by Marianne Evers.

Doulton stoneware kangaroo umbrella stand, 1885.

University of Sydney. These buildings are probably the finest examples of Australian sandstone architecture in the Gothic style and it is interesting, given the intensely English atmosphere that this first Australian university was intended to promote, that kangaroos were chosen to take the place of the griffins, lizards, pards and lions rampant that would have adorned a similar building in the old country. The specific mission of the university to provide a seat of higher learning for the sons of the new colonists and thus prevent the need for them to go back to Oxford or Cambridge is, through these figures, symbolically

Kangaroo gargoyle
at Sydney University,
c. 2010.

reinforced in a tension by which buildings that look like Oxbridge colleges are given a specifically Australian identity and located in an Australian space by the very simple technique of grafting a kangaroo onto the roof line.

Other examples are provided by two stamps. A one-shilling stamp was produced in 1888 as part of a series to mark the centenary of the foundation of the colony, then state, of New South Wales. It shows a kangaroo in a pose deriving from the Stubbs painting but delineated, by the designer Henry Barraclough, with a good deal of naturalistic accuracy. This stamp, harmless though it may seem now, caused significant controversy when it was released. Not only was it innovative in showing an animal

Australian troops en route to the Boer War with their kangaroo mascot, c. 1899.

rather than a person (possibly the first stamp to do so in phila-
telic history) but it also omitted the head of Queen Victoria.

In 1913, when it was agreed that the post-federation Australian
states should no longer issue their own stamps, the first approved
design for a national stamp consisted of a map of Australia with
a kangaroo superimposed. This again caused controversy because
it omitted the head of King George v and was subsequently
replaced by a more conventional design featuring the monarch.
The kangaroo is here not only the unambiguous bearer of the
message that these are Australian stamps, but also, for one of the
first times, a bearer of messages about the future of Australia, its
sense of independent nationhood and its potential governance.
It is, perhaps, ironic that when the early settlers wanted to
cement particular relationships with Indigenous peoples they
created kings who bore the image of the kangaroo on their

An Australian kangaroo stamp from 1913.

A kangaroo mascot with convalescent Anzac troops in the UK, 1916.

metal gorgets, but when the early nationalists wished to signal their intentions concerning their relationship with their own king they issued stamps with kangaroos on them. Either way, the kangaroo stands out as the most naturally appropriated symbol of specifically Australian intentions.

Throughout the twentieth century the kangaroo bore symbolic burdens, not least as a part of military campaigns. The first major war effort the Australians undertook was the expeditionary force that was sent in support of British and other imperial contingents in the second campaign against the Boers from 1899 to 1902 (although units from the Australian states had earlier served in the Sudan and were also part of the multinational force sent to put down the Boxer Uprising in China – where six men are still buried – in 1900 and 1901). This reinforced both the sense of a specific Australian identity and

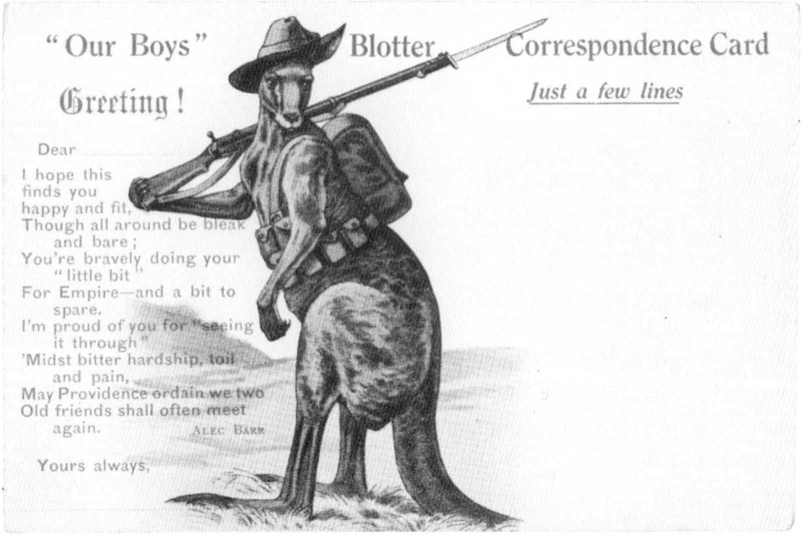
"Our Boys" Blotter Correspondence Card
Greeting!
Just a few lines
Dear
I hope this
finds you
happy and fit,
Though all around be bleak
and bare;
You're bravely doing your
"little bit"
For Empire—and a bit to
spare.
I'm proud of you for "seeing
it through"
'Midst bitter hardship, toil
and pain,
May Providence ordain we two
Old friends shall often meet
again.
ALEC BARR
Yours always,

'Our Boys' postcard from the First World War.

the close links that still existed between Australia and the British Empire. The more traumatic events of 1914 to 1918 both strengthened and challenged this complex conceptual linkage almost to the point of breakage. It is often said that an independent Australian identity was first fully formed on the beaches and cliffs of Gallipoli, but Australian troops were also deployed in force on the Western Front and at least one historian of the Flanders and French campaigns, Roland Perry, has claimed that it was the Australian contribution to the great counter-offensives of 1918 under the generalship of Sir John Monash that actually won the war (which was always going to depend on the outcome of the campaign in Europe) for the Allied side.[3] Certainly, Australian soldiers were frequently used as shock troops and their victories were achieved at a disproportionate cost in Australian lives even when they were fully under Australian command and operating with a high degree of autonomy.

The kangaroo begins to turn up in the popular iconography of the war very early on and a common image, which was used on a number of different ephemera (greetings cards, etc.), showed the creature dressed in the classic uniform of the digger, complete with the distinctive slouch hat, doing its patriotic duty at the front. Kangaroos were also commonly used in recruitment posters and propaganda posters to stress the importance of Australian participation in the war – which was by no means unanimously supported at the political level as the campaigns dragged on – as part of the cement which bound the country to Britain and the Empire. Here the kangaroo is placed between two political and cultural impulses. It is both the symbol of a proudly independent and characteristically Australian national identity and the bridge by which that identity can be negotiated

A kangaroo helps military recruitment in this poster of 1915.

A nurse at a First World War hospital in the UK for Australian Auxiliaries, with their kangaroo mascot Jimony.

in a continuing relationship with the empire and the old country. In this respect the immensely complex Australian reaction to the war and its aftermath (the issue of commemoration and the treatment of the Australian war dead, for example, was so problematic that it was not until 1993 that Australia repatriated a body from a First World War grave as an 'unknown soldier'),

Kangaroo in Khartoum Zoo, 1936.

in which mourning and pride mingled with doubt as to the good faith with which the immense Australian sacrifice had been received in Britain, is borne by these very simple images.

This doubt was amplified during the Second World War by the anxiety over a possible Japanese invasion while the Australian main force was committed to supporting imperial forces overseas. Even so, during this war the kangaroo took on a less complex burden as the mascot of various Australian units including an armoured brigade and several Air Force squadrons. Individual planes also bore the image of the kangaroo, such as the Second World War ace Wing-Commander Bobby Gibbes's Kittyhawk fighter which featured his mother's design of a kangaroo kicking a dachshund. The ships of the Royal Australian Navy still have kangaroos painted on them and the roundels of the Royal Australian Air Force have a red kangaroo in the centre.

The Australian Imperial Forces during the Great War played
their part in spreading the image of the kangaroo around the
world and, in addition, they left kangaroos almost wherever they
went. Kangaroos from Australian units based in Egypt found
their way to Cairo Zoo, for example, and this facility built up a

disproportionately large collection of Australian animals in the years that followed. The zoo finally ran out of kangaroos in 1990, but more arrived at this notoriously neglected facility in 2009 and their current condition must give cause for concern. More poignantly, during the Second World War, Australian nurses in Japanese hands in the Dutch East Indies found the daily humiliation of being forced to bow to the Japanese flag was greatly lessened by attaching a home-made kangaroo called Josephine to the flagpole.[4]

One feature of Australian culture is the centrality of sport and the expectation that Australians and Australian teams will excel in international competition. This is a feature from colonial times and the England–Australia cricket series known as the Ashes is one of the oldest continuous sporting competitions in the world (although it can be forgotten that the first Australian cricket team to tour England was not the first official team in 1878 but an all-Aboriginal team that visited to enormous applause in 1868). Australian teams frequently have kangaroo or kangaroo-derived names, for example, the Wallabies (who play rugby union), the Kangaroos (rugby league), the Socceroos (association football), the Jillaroos (women's rugby league), the Boomers (mens's basketball) the Hockeyroos (women's hockey), the Jackaroos (men's bowls), the Mighty Roos (men's ice hockey), the Joeys (under-17 men's association football) and the Wheelabies (wheelchair rugby). In these instances the kangaroo bears not only the weight of national identity, but also the hope and expectation that its durability and strength will somehow transfer to the players. In this respect we see a rare and entirely unacknowledged connection between mainstream contemporary Australian society and traditional Indigenous beliefs.

Perhaps the most celebrated example of the kangaroo being pressed into sporting service is the boxing kangaroo flag developed

for Alan Bond's successful America's Cup challenge with his yacht *Australia II* in 1983. The importance of this event to Australia and Australians is not well understood overseas (except perhaps in the yachting communities of the US). Its significance was noted again within Australia when in 2009 the original Bond flag (which had been hanging in a bar on Rhode Island since the race) was returned to Australia where it can now be seen in the excellent Maritime Museum in Fremantle. This flag and variants of it have become common sights at Australian sporting events and it has now been adopted as the official flag of the Australian Olympic Committee.

In the depiction of the boxing kangaroo in sporting (and to a lesser extent, military) contexts we see another interesting duality. The pugnacity of the kangaroo (and although kangaroos are not normally aggressive they have the strength and armoury to inflict very considerable damage on soft tissue, although there

JUMPING TO A CONCLUSION.

appears to be only one attested case of someone being killed by a kangaroo) is always tempered by the cartoon-like and inevitably friendly image that is depicted on the various flags and posters. It is almost as if there is a reluctance to disclose fully the aggression that is required for sporting success and a tempering of the competitive edge in favour of stressing the social nature of sport and the way it brings together different kinds of people for a common purpose. Australian sport has always prided itself on the way in which it offers a very public showcase for the main Australian value of fairness and here the image of the kangaroo bears that burden in its transformation into something entirely unthreatening. In addition, the depiction of the feisty but non-aggressive kangaroo denies the earlier colonial image of the animal as a dangerous creature that will attack unprovoked and will certainly fight back when approached, which was used so extensively in the nineteenth century to justify its hunting for sport.

Kangaroos have always formed part of the settler Australian diet (albeit an occasionally controversial part) and Indigenous Australians have respected the kangaroo as a worthy creature to be both revered within totemic and kinship systems and to be hunted with due respect. In colonial times kangaroo formed both a necessary dietary standby on the frontier and became a delicacy. In 1864 Edward Abbott produced *The English and Australian Cookery Book: Cookery for the Many as Well as the Upper Ten Thousand by an Australian Aristologist* in which he gave this recipe for kangaroo steamer:

Take the most tender part of the kangaroo, being careful to remove all the sinews. Chop it very fine, about the same quantity of smoked bacon (fat), season with finely powdered marjoram, pepper and a very little salt. Let it steam or stew for two hours; then pack or press tight in open-mouthed glass bottles; the bung must be sealed down, and the outside of the bottles washed well with white of egg, beaten; preserved in this way it will keep 'good' [I find those quotation marks ominous!] for twelve months

Kangaroo sauce advertisement, 1890s.

or more. When needed for use, the vessel containing the preserve should be put into a saucepan of cold water, and allowed to boil for fifteen minutes (if a large bottle); when dished pour a little rich brown gravy over it, flavoured with mace, salt and pepper; garnish with forcemeat. If required for immediate use, half an hour will cook it sufficiently; no gravy will be necessary. Forcemeat balls without bacon will be found a great improvement.[5]

This is no ordinary steamer recipe, as it derives from the dish that won Mrs Sarah Crouch, 'the lady of the respected Under-Sheriff of Tasmania', a prize medal at the London Exhibition of 1862. Interestingly, this very same dish was served at the 1862 London dinner of the Acclimatisation Society. The eminent Sir John Maxwell 'pronounced it excellent, as a stew and said that he would like to see it introduced into the Navy.' So delicious was this recipe that Abbott added:

It is understood that Prince Napoleon, one of the first gastronomers of the day, was desirous to acclimatize kangaroo to France, for the sake of the 'cuisine' [those quote marks again . . .] the animal affords.

This book contains no less than nine kangaroo recipes in all: ham, hashed, jugged, pan jam (ash-roasted tails fried with bacon and mushrooms), pasty, roast, steamer and stuffing. The most alarming is the peculiarly Australian 'slippery bob':

Take kangaroo brains, and mix with flour and water, and make into batter; well season with pepper, salt etc; then pour a table-spoonful at a time into an iron pot containing emeu [sic] fat, and take them out when done. 'Bush fare,' requiring a good appetite and excellent digestion.

Indeed. Even a good glass of Penfold's Grange might make this one hard to get down (pan jam isn't much better but it is made from tails not brains so is probably more palatable).

'Buy Australian sultanas', part of an Empire Marketing Board campaign to sell Australian produce in Britain, *c.* 1919, artist Frederick C. Herrick.

Hilda M. Freeman's memoir *Murrumbidgee Memories and Riverina Reminiscences: A Collection of Old Bush History*, written in the 1930s, speaks of the excitement of kangaroo hunting – with the ladies all riding side-saddle – and the practical results of a successful run:

> Kangaroo tail soup was really very good, and many a meal was supplied by meat cut from the loin of a kangaroo. Strangers often enjoyed this meal, not knowing what it was.

This was in the 1870s. Kangaroo eating has still not found widespread acceptance in Australia so it has been left to gourmands and tourists to lead the way. The menus of the top restaurants of Sydney have replaced the Great Dividing Range or the Blue Mountains as the great Australian challenge.

Interestingly, *The English and Australian Cookery Book* also offers some thoughts on the nature of kangaroos which give insight into attitudes in early Australia and reinforces the opinion that kangaroos can be much more dangerous than they actually are:

> Usually mild inoffensive animals, they are sometimes stirred up to wrath when brought to bay by dogs; and there are two instances on record in the Bothwell district, of 'boomers' (forester kangaroos) having seized men in their arms, and carried them for some distance and then flung them violently down.

Certainly, kangaroos are big strong animals, but although there are reports of kangaroo attacks in gardens and even on golf courses, only one reliably documented case of a human fatality from a kangaroo attack exists. That incident dates from 1936 when a hunter in New South Wales was killed by a kangaroo while trying to rescue his dogs.

Sexual encounters between kangaroos and human beings are also virtually unknown, but in May 2010 a sexually excited kangaroo started to pester women in the remote Northern Territory town of Tennant Creek. Tanya Wilson encountered him at a speedway race meeting and here is her story:

> I thought it was strange that a kangaroo would come to such a noisy place, but I grew up around kangaroos so I

went up to say hello. There I was having a nice chat to him when I heard others calling out to me, warning me to step away. I didn't take any notice of them because I didn't think I had anything to worry about – I thought he was just a cute, friendly kangaroo.[6]

The *Northern Territory News* now takes up the tale:

But other speedway fans could tell what the roo wanted and when one man tried to intervene he was punched in the face by the animal before it hopped off.[7]

Nellie Melba meets a kangaroo, 1902.

A year later the kangaroo was still making news and was stalking female joggers in the Tennant Creek area.[8] In July 2011, 94-year-old Phyllis Johnson of Charleville, Queensland, was pegging out her washing when she was attacked by Eddie, an escaped pet kangaroo. Nonagenarians are made of stern stuff in Queensland and she fought the kangaroo with her broom until the local police came and doused it with pepper spray.[9]

Australian culture has always been able to appropriate the kangaroo for almost any symbolic service that is required. Since the 1950s the kangaroo has also been used to attract people to come to Australia either as tourists or migrants. Most famously, the national airline, Qantas, features a stylized kangaroo on the tails of its fleet. This kangaroo speaks not only for the national identity of an Australian airline but also, in its dynamic, almost deco-like design, stresses the speed and agility of the Qantas planes as they leap from city to city and from continent to continent. Trans Australia Airlines (founded in 1946 and taken over wholly by Qantas in 1996) also had a stylized kangaroo as its logo. The Australia Council for the Arts uses a kangaroo, too – which looks as if it derives from Indigenous Australian rock art – as the main element of its logo. However, things can go wrong.

In 2010 Tourism Australia created a media frenzy when they displayed a live kangaroo in a cage in Los Angeles as one of the attractions of the G'Day USA advertising campaign.[10] Video footage shows the kangaroo crouching and swaying in what appears to be distress. Tourism Australia defended their position and claimed that the kangaroo was always supervised by professional handlers and that the American Humane Association had confirmed that the animal was not in distress. This did not, however, convince many Australians who took the opportunity to say some interesting things about kangaroos. These comments

An Australian
tourist poster
from 1957.

Qantas Boeing 'wallabies'.

draw attention to the perception of the exceptional character of the kangaroo:

'Mr McEvoy said that America Humane – the USA equivalent of Australia's RSPCA – had seen the video and said the animal was not in distress.' How the hell would they know if a kangaroo was in distress . . . Probably just as much as I know a moose or bison would be in distress.

The American Humane Society would know very little about macropod physiology and to use this assessment as an excuse sounds a bit desperate to me. If they bothered to find out about the effects of stress on kangaroos they would know that it can bring about a condition known as myopathy . . . and the animal dies a month later never

ever showing any obvious signs of distress. I think our most famous emblem deserves a little more respect . . .'[11]

Of course, Tourism Australia uses a kangaroo as the main feature of its logo.

Finally, there was a significant growth in Australian design especially in the immediate post-war period. Following the lead set by artists like Margaret Preston, the designs often appropriated Indigenous motifs or Indigenous themes. Ethleen Palmer produced a number of linocuts and screen prints featuring Australian motifs including some fine stylized kangaroos. Annie Outlaw and Nance Mackenzie of Annan Fabrics produced similar images in materials designed for furniture coverings or curtains. The art pottery of Merric Boyd also featured Australian animals including kangaroos, while, on a more popular note, the Vande Pottery produced some striking images of Indigenous Australians (which would not pass muster today) as well as pieces that featured kangaroos.[12]

At this time, both Australian design and the Australian economy were at a point of transition. The old dependency on Britain could no longer be relied on and the idea of importing goods that featured Australian motifs – as in the case of the Doulton pieces mentioned above – became less palatable to a society that was increasingly (especially after what was widely seen as a betrayal in the surrender of Singapore to the Japanese in 1942) developing a sense of cultural and political independence. In addition, slowly changing attitudes to Indigenous Australians and the beginnings of white interest in Indigenous art and culture meant that purely Australian designs could make a case in a market that was still largely protected by high-tariff barriers. Kangaroos had been a feature of Australian decorative arts for many years, of course, and in the 1930s had featured in the output

FATHER CHRISTMAS IN AUSTRALIA.

of the Melrose Pottery and also in the more utilitarian Fowler Ware. But in the 1950s the use of Australian design motifs, especially images of kangaroos, whether in the studio tradition of Boyd or the mass-produced Diana Ware pottery, became much more a statement of a specific national identity and less a superficial decorative feature to denote Australian origin.

9.

4 The Kangaroo Abroad

Even today kangaroos are sufficiently odd to make it worth exhibiting them; we saw in chapter Three how Tourism Australia got itself into a steamer with its unwise display of a kangaroo in Beverly Hills. In the same year (2010) the Internet search company Google also made the news with their New York office's Take Your Child to Work Day event, which included the display of a live kangaroo in a cage. Inevitably this was filmed; inevitably the footage went on the Internet; and inevitably the allegations concerning the mistreatment and stressing of the kangaroo began to fly. Google claimed, equally inevitably, that the animal was not mistreated because it was supervised by professional hand-lers, and a spokesperson from Google Australia – presumably it was felt in New York that the Australians knew their kangaroos – was wheeled out to argue rather extraordinarily, but with commendable ingenuity, that the kangaroo was not in a cage anyway because the four barred walls that surrounded it did not have a roof.[1]

But why should Google have thought that a kangaroo would be just the thing to amuse the children? My guess is that the answer lies in the fact that the Google staff were brought up on the American children's programme *Captain Kangaroo*, probably the longest-running series of its kind, which was screened from

Red-necked wallaby (*Macropus rufogriseus*) shaking its head.

137

late 1955 until late 1984 and then again in a series of reruns with new material from 1986 until 1993. An unsuccessful *All New Captain Kangaroo* also had a brief life for one season in 1997 and 1998. The younger Google workers would also have been familiar with the 'K for Kangaroo' segment from the long-running *Sesame Street* and with Kasey the Kangaroo from *Jim Henson's Animal Show*. So it would have seemed a perfect choice for the entertainment of a new generation.

But to find kangaroo exhibitions in Britain you have to go back at least two centuries. In 1790 the people of Scotland were presented with a new sensation when Alexander Weir, owner of the Museum of Natural Curiosities, announced the arrival and exhibition of:

> The extraordinary quadruped called the CUNQUROO . . . being the first that was ever brought to Britain.

It is unclear whether this animal was alive or dead, because the next year, in November 1791, London was presented with an even newer sensation when the public – or those members of the public that could afford the very stiff one-shilling entry fee – were treated to the exhibition of a new animal: The Wonderful Kangaroo from Botany Bay. This was promoted in *The Times* as follows:

> The Wonderful Kangaroo from Botany Bay. A most beautiful and healthy animal in a state of perfect tameness, and entirely free from any blemish, is now exhibiting at no.31, the top of the Hay Market. Admittance One shilling each. It is not easy to describe that peculiarity of attitudes and uncommon proportion of parts which so strikingly distinguishes the Kangaroo from all other Creatures; and

THE KANGAROO.
Drawn from the Animal in the Possession of Mr. Stockdale, Piccadilly.
Published as the Act directs 1st Nov.r 1790, by I. Stockdale, Picca.

Peter Mazell, 'The Kangaroo. Drawn from the Animal in the Possession of Mr Stockdale, Piccadilly', illustration for the *Literary Magazine and British Review* (1790).

it may be presumed, that few who possess a taste for science or a laudable curiousity of inspecting Wonders of Nature, will resist embracing the only opportunity hitherto afforded in Europe of viewing this singular Native of the Southern Hemisphere, in its natural state of vigour and activity.

It was clearly a great success and it would appear that three years later, what I assume was the same creature was exhibited again:

The Wonderful Kanguroo from Botany Bay (the only One ever brought alive to Europe) to be seen at the LYCEUM, in the Strand from 8 in the morning till 8 in the evening. This amazing, beautiful and tame Animal, is about five Feet in Height, of a Fawn colour, and distinguished itself in Shape, Make and true Symmetry of Parts, *different from all other QUADRUPEDS*. Its swiftness when pursued is superior to the GREYHOUND: to enumerate its extraordinary Qualities would far exceed the common Limits of a Public Notice. Let it suffice to observe, that the public in general are pleased, and bestow their plaudits; the Ingenious are delighted; the Virtuoso, and Connoisseur are taught to admire! Impressing the Beholder with Wonder and Astonishment, at the sight of this unparalleled animal from the Southern Hemisphere that almost surpasses belief; therefore Ocular Demonstration will exceed all that words can describe, or Pencil delineate – Admittance ONE SHILLING each.

The similarity of the advertisement and the claim that is the first kangaroo in Europe suggests that it was the same animal. Notice also how the second advertisement picks up some of Banks's descriptive terminology and the all-important comparison with the greyhound.

However, interestingly, there was even more to see. The copy of the advertisement that is now kept in the archives of the National Library of Australia in Canberra has some handwritten comments on it from someone who actually went to the exhibition:

> I saw it and was surprised to find the view annexd, taken at a glance, so very near accuracy. W. Br. A very pleasing lively creature died in 1796 or 1799.

So clearly there was, in addition to the live animal, a picture. Was this the Stubbs painting? More probably it was a copy of the painting or some other representation, the identity of which is now lost to us. But how was the exhibition staged? Did you see the picture of the kangaroo and then the kangaroo itself? Or did you see the kangaroo and the picture together, so that the objective of the show was not only to introduce you to a zoological marvel but also to show off a piece of virtuoso life drawing (hence the reference to the pencil in the advertisement)? How the show worked is no longer known. We do know that the 1791 exhibition included the opportunity to see the animal led around, so we should assume that the same obtained in the second show, but it is interesting how, even when a live specimen was available, there was clearly a desire, an anxiety even, to demonstrate that this was an animal that could be represented and, maybe, that the representations that had thus far been available in England – even when they came from such unimpeachable sources as Cook and Banks – were of a real animal and not the fantasy of travellers or colonial boosters seeking to talk up the wonders of the new British lands in the far south.

The idea that one could substitute a picture for a live animal was not new to the European imagination. In the early 1750s Christian Ludwig ii of Mecklenburg-Schwerin had commissioned the

Yellow-footed rock wallaby (*Petrogale xanthopus*) at Monarto Zoological Park, South Australia.

French painter Jean-Baptiste Oudry to produce for him just such a menagerie to enable him to compete with grander aristocrats whose deeper purses offered them the opportunity to own the real thing. The animals that Oudry used as his models were the classiest of all in that they were kept in Louis xv's royal menagerie at Versailles.[2] Nor is the idea that the kangaroo was some kind of fake necessarily far-fetched. This was precisely the fate of the platypus, which was widely supposed to be a taxidermic fraud (not unreasonably, since such fantasy animals were not uncommon, perhaps the most famous being Captain Eades's mermaid, which could be seen for a shilling at London's Turf Coffeehouse in 1822). Even an exhibited platypus specimen at the Great Exhibition – stuffed by the great John Gould himself – seems not to have dispelled the doubts fully.[3]

Whatever the reality of the exhibition's organization, it is clear that the showing of this kangaroo was by no means a straightforward event and you got good value for your shilling. The statement in the anonymous viewer's note that the kangaroo died some two to five years later raises the question of where it went after the show. Was it one of the kangaroos living on Banks's estate at Revesby, for example? It may well have been

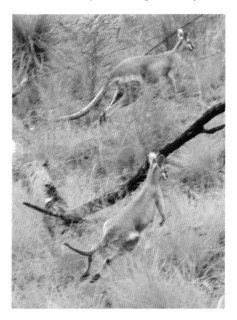

Whiptail wallaby (*Macropus parryi*).

moved to the Exeter 'Change, a great menagerie in the centre of London, where all manner of surprisingly exotic animals could be seen. This establishment eventually succumbed to the trend by which the display of such creatures declined as a rowdy working-class form of entertainment and was replaced by the middle-class and educational zoological garden. This decline was probably hastened by the notorious slaying in 1826 of the great elephant Chunee who went wild, presumably while in must, and was killed by fusillades of shots from a detachment of soldiers and a pike thrust from his keeper. We know that by 1793 there were kangaroos in the 'Change but if this specimen was one of them does this mean that it was not the same animal as the one that was exhibited in 1791 (which seems overwhelmingly likely)?

But was the kangaroo really the first to be seen live in England? Temptingly, an advertisement for a wild animal show in Norwich in 1783 included, together with a tiger, a lion, a porcupine, a wolf and a 'moon act' (possibly a chimpanzee), 'A Beautiful Creature called a Wanderoo, Being the only one of that Species ever seen in Europe'. This may, possibly, have been a wallaroo, but was almost certainly a kind of monkey. We do not always know from these early advertisements whether the exhibits were of live animals or stuffed ones. One of the irritations to visitors to the Crystal Palace in 1851 was that the associated menagerie was, in fact, entirely composed of stuffed specimens. It is very likely that stuffed kangaroos and wallabies had made their way to England by 1783. Certainly by 1795 a London taxidermist was advertising his wares with a medallion showing a kangaroo (based on the Stubbs painting), an armadillo and a rhinoceros (a distant legacy of Dürer's wonderful image), and similar images – including a Stubbsian kangaroo – can be found on the tokens made by Gilbert Pidcock for entry into his London menagerie between 1795 and 1801.

Joseph Banks certainly was keeping kangaroos on his Lincoln-shire estate at Revesby by the 1790s and there were kangaroos in the royal menagerie at Windsor Great Park by 1793. Queen Charlotte was keeping kangaroos (together with many other pets) in the grounds of what is now known as Queen Charlotte's Cottage in Kew Gardens – a kind of non-threatening version of Marie Antoinette's Petit Trianon. These bred very successfully, as did the other kangaroos in the royal collections, well into the nineteenth century. Royal specimens were also exhibited at the other royal zoo in the Tower of London. An early advertisement for that venerable establishment makes it very clear that the kangaroos that were displayed there were home grown ('bred in Windsor Great Park'). In 1800, when George III's daughter, Princess Charlotte, Duchess of Württemberg, found herself marooned in the barren Franconian country estate of Erlangen, her access to her court being cut off by the Napoleonic wars, she sent home for two kangaroos to keep her company.[4] In the late nineteenth century another aristocratic menagerie keeper, the Duke of Marlborough, was experimenting with kangaroos at Blenheim, although it appears that segregating this mob from his prized pack of hounds proved a daily trial. The Earl of Derby had a very significant menagerie at Knowsley Hall in Lancashire (ironically, this is now a safari park). This was dispersed in 1851 and the catalogue of the sale shows that it included numerous kangaroos of a range of species. Many of these were bought up by the major dealers in exotic animals, Jamrach and Cross. Edward Lear (who had begun his career as a wildlife illustrator working not very happily for John Gould on the *Birds of Europe* project) spent three happy years drawing the animals at Knowl-sey and seventeen of his paintings were reproduced in a luxury volume, *Gleanings from the Menagerie and Aviary at Knowsley Hall* (1846). An earlier painting of a newly discovered kangaroo species,

Macropus parryi (commonly known as the whiptail wallaby), was published in the *Transactions of the Zoological Society of London* for 1835.

The royal tradition of kangaroo keeping was maintained when Prince Alfred, Duke of Edinburgh, embarked on his world cruise in his ship HMS *Galatea* between 1868 and 1870 with a break in 1869 when he had to return to England after having been the victim of a Fenian assassination attempt in Sydney. The prince was the first member of the royal family to visit Australia (indeed the first to cross the Equator) and along the way he visited India

The whiptail wallaby (*Macropus parryi*), lithograph after a watercolour by Edward Lear in *Transactions of the Zoological Society of London*, vol. I (1835).

and South Africa. The prince did a good deal of hunting and his exploits were the subject of regular reporting in *The Times*. He was also a collector of animals and shipped many back to England with him. These included an elephant and a significant Australian menagerie including kangaroos. In 1869 he had a wombat which I believe subsequently passed into the hands of the Pre-Raphaelite painter Dante Gabriel Rossetti. Prince Alfred sent his animals to London Zoo because the glory days of royal menagerie keeping were, alas, past.[5] A *Punch* cartoon from 1868 by the renowned John Tenniel (illustrator of *Alice's Adventures in Wonderland*) showed a dapper and uniformed Prince Alfred shaking hands with a strapping 'Australian Cousin' (who is significantly taller than he is). She is dressed as a quasi-rococo shepherdess and has a flock of sheep behind her, but she is leading a kangaroo on a ribbon. The accompanying text is a letter from Britannia to Australia which ends:

> P.S. (Woman-like) I have addressed you by your usual name, but properly, you know, you ought to be styled Australasia. So let it be Floreat Australasia! Have you any pet name? What say you to Kangarooia?[6]

It's a shame that didn't catch on.

Dr Johnson's *A Dictionary of the English Language* (1755) was published before the English knew that there were kangaroos in Australia, but the great man was, in later life, not immune to the seductions of Antipodean wildlife. He had a description of the kangaroo given to him by Sir Joseph Banks himself and this clearly made a deep impression. Perhaps a deeper impression than Banks himself, for although the two men met many times and Banks was, in fact, one of the pall-bearers at Johnson's funeral, Johnson found Banks callow and arrogant. As he said to Mrs Thrale: 'You may remember: I thought Banks had not gained much by circumnavigating the world.' However, Banks had left his mark and when Johnson was on his famous tour of Scotland in 1773 he fell in with the Reverend Alexander Grant and some others at Mackenzie's Inn in Inverness and the talk turned to kangaroos. The ever-faithful biographer Boswell describes what happened next:

He [Dr Johnson] stood erect, put out his hands like feelers,
and, gathering up the tails of his huge brown coat so as
to resemble the pouch of the animal, made two or three
vigorous bounds across the room.[7]

What an astonishing sight that must have been!

Many attempts were made to bring live kangaroos back to
the British Isles. For example, when the great reforming governor
of New South Wales, Lachlan Macquarie, came home to Scotland in 1822, we know that among the many souvenirs of his
Australian sojourn were seven kangaroos (together with six emus,
seven black swans, four Cape Barren geese, two native compan-
ions[!], one 'Narang emu', two white cockatoos, two bronze-wing
pigeons, four wanga-wanga pigeons and several parrots and
lowries [lorikeets] which, unfortunately, died on the voyage). This
was not an uncommon happening since by the 1820s the colony
was well established and animals were frequently being shipped
back to the old country. In 1819, for example, the returning convict James Hardy Vaux noted that the ship he was travelling on
'resembled a Noah's Ark. There were kangaroos, black swans, a
noble emu, and cockatoos, parrots and smaller birds without
number.' They all died on the voyage except one cockatoo and
some swans.

My opinion (the mysterious wanderoo notwithstanding) is
that the London kangaroo may well have been the first to reach
England alive, but whatever the truth of the matter, the kangaroo had already entered the English poetic imagination. We first
find one in Anna Seward's 'Elegy on Captain Cook':

Next Fauna treads, in youthful Beauty's Pride,
A playful Kangaroo bounding by her side
Around the Nymph her beauteous Pois display

Their varied plumes and trill the dulcet lay;
A Giant-bat, with leathern wings outspread,
Umbrella light, hangs quiv'ring o'er her head.

Here the kangaroo takes its place in a procession designed simultaneously to display the wonders of Cook's discoveries and to locate Cook in a mythologized landscape that would have been familiar to Seward's readers, who, if they did not have a classical education themselves, would have been at home with and have expected a stock of imagery that offered a classical reference even when the underlying theme was Australia where, presumably, the Olympian gods never strayed. When Sir Walter Scott edited the works in 1810 he added a footnote as follows:

> The kangaroo is an animal peculiar to these climates. It is perpetually jumping along on its hind legs, its fore legs being too short to be used in the manner of other quadrupeds.

This, I suspect, was unnecessary because it is likely that by this time, everyone who was sufficiently wealthy to have access to a book of verse such as Seward's would probably have known what a kangaroo was and would have seen, if nothing else, the engraving of the Stubbs painting. Notice also how Scott appears to be drawing on Banks for his description.

The next emergence of a kangaroo in English poetry is to be found in 'Elinor', one of Robert Southey's *Botany Bay Eclogues* (1794):

> And for the music of the bleating flocks,
> Alone is heard the kangaroo's sad note
> Deepening in the distance.

The red kangaroo (*Macropus rufus*) by Joseph Wolf, from his *Zoological Sketches* (1861).

The kangaroo provides a sign of the desolate mournfulness of the Australian landscape and Southey gives it a voice to add to the general sense of desperation. He speaks of a 'pathless' landscape which contrasts with the cultivated English landscape of memory inhabited by 'fearless redbreasts'. Ironically, had the poem been written 50 years later, all sound would have been drowned out by the bleating of the giant merino sheep on whose backs Australians rode to wealth. One wonders, incidentally, if the reference to a redbreast is an ironic comment on the Bow Street Runners who may well have effected the arrests that led to many transportations. They were in existence by 1750 and although they did not wear a uniform, there is a suggestion (which was only confirmed as late as 1862 by Dickens and, therefore, may be his invention) that they favoured red waistcoats and, therefore, were known as Robin Redbreasts. This could well be a nice little joke on Southey's part, and if it really is a reference to the Bow Street Runners it offers a much earlier confirmation that they did wear red waistcoats (if that is why they were called Redbreasts) than any other found. But it is obvious that Southey had little idea what a kangaroo was or how it behaved. It is likely that he would have read Cook or Banks – every educated gentleman of this period did – but he clearly had not forked out his shilling to see the animal in the Haymarket or the Lyceum. So the kangaroo takes its place as part of the paraphernalia of exotica denoting the strangeness of the Australian landscape.

By the middle of the nineteenth century kangaroos had become very familiar to the British, so much so that in *David Copperfield* Charles Dickens has Mr Micawber refer to 'the habits of the kangaroo'. He would not have done this unless he was fairly certain that his audience would know what he was talking about. By this time, kangaroos were to be seen not only in the zoological gardens but also in the many travelling menageries that toured the British Isles and offered people in the most far-flung reaches of the county the opportunity to see a huge range of exotic animals, including, of course, kangaroos. The establishment of an Australian literary culture at about the same time meant that kangaroos were becoming common in poetry, but in 1804 in Britain the idea of the kangaroo was still bearing the burden of strangeness as evidenced by this passage from Charles Dibdin's bizarre work *The Harmonic Preceptor: A Didactic Poem in Three Parts*, which was an attempt to versify the principles of musical composition:

> Modern singing, were't not to true taste so injurious,
> Might be really encouraged like anything curious,
> An invisible girl, or a young kangaroo,
> Or pigs without heads, or a calf that has two,
> A hare beating a drum, or a crocodile stuffed,
> Or any thing else the news-papers have puffed,

Which obtains on the public by sly advertising,
And are really wonderful thought, and surprising.

I have no doubt that here Dibdin had, very much at the fore-
front of his mind, the kind of discourse that we saw in the
advertisements for the Haymarket and Lyceum exhibitions; even
ten to fifteen years later, when there was regular connection
between England and Australia (and, therefore, a regular supply
of kangaroos), he still felt that he could employ the idea of the
kangaroo as an image for strangeness alongside taxidermic wonders and fairground freaks.

Towards the end of the nineteenth century the most famous
kangaroo keeper was probably Lord Walter Rothschild, who kept
an enormous menagerie at his country estate at Tring Park which
included a number of kangaroos. Rothschild was a wonderful
eccentric who rode in a landau drawn by zebras and was pictured
riding a giant tortoise, urging it on by means of a lettuce attached
to fishing rod.[8] One of his kangaroos caused mayhem at Euston
Station when it escaped and made off down the platform.

In the twentieth century the spirit of Revesby was revived by
a pair of kangaroos that lived in a private garden in Lincoln and,
on occasion, vexed the local police and convinced local drunks
to sign the pledge by making off and hopping around the town.
The garden they lived in was overlooked by the old Lincoln hospital and, most specifically, by the labour ward of its maternity
unit; I have spoken to a number of now-elderly Lincolnshire
ladies who vividly remember watching the kangaroos hopping
about while they were having their babies. I imagine this must
have encouraged them in their efforts.[9]

A celebrated kangaroo was the 'boxing kangaroo' displayed by
'Professor' Landerman at the Royal Aquarium in London in 1892
and 1893. Sarah Bernhardt herself enjoyed this entertainment.

Boxing kangaroos have, since the earliest period of European–kangaroo encounters formed part of the entertainment scene and were the focus of two early films, which were presumably inspired by the cult of Landerman's kangaroo. These were a German film, *Das Boxende Känguruh,* directed by Max Skladanowsky in 1895 and an English film, *The Boxing Kangaroo*, which was directed by Birt Acres in 1896. In 1920 the American director Dave Fleischer made an animated short also entitled *The Boxing Kangaroo*. A Pathé newsreel from 1930 shows a boxing kangaroo display in Cape Town that ends badly when the kangaroo attacks a female spectator. The boxing behaviour is natural in male kangaroos, who do appear to box when they fight, and although the intent is more defensive than aggressive, a kangaroo can inflict serious injury because it has exceptionally sharp claws and enormous strength in its legs. Boxing kangaroo shows still exist

Wallabies fighting.

154

and are the object of much outrage from animal welfare campaigners, especially when the kangaroo is dressed up. In 2010 police investigated an incident at a party in a hotel in Dublin where a kangaroo was released onto the dance floor and, it is alleged, subsequently died.[10]

Interestingly, it was a boxing kangaroo that gave occasion to the testing of the Married Women's Property Act as it applied in Australia when, in 1891, the Supreme Court of New South Wales heard a case in which Mrs Olivia Mayne sued the McMahon brothers for the money they owed her for the hire of her boxing kangaroo 'Fighting Jack'. This kangaroo was a well-known Australian figure and a model of him was to be seen attracting crowds in the Melbourne Waxworks at the time of the trial. The case (which Mrs Mayne won) concerned the capability of a married woman to enter into a contract, but it gives us a fascinating, if fleeting, glimpse of the life of a celebrity kangaroo. Jack died in 1891 and

Black, or swamp wallaby (*Wallabia bicolor*, ex *Halmaturus ualabatus*).

the *Newcastle Morning Herald and Miners' Advocate* ran an obituary for him, describing him as 'an ambitious young kangaroo pugilist'. Jack's handler, a Mr von Lindeman, appears to have been the same person as the 'Professor' Landerman who turned up in London a year later with the boxing kangaroo at the aquarium.[11]

Sporting kangaroos are also known in other contexts and one urban myth, which continues to be propagated today, concerns a kangaroo in a coat. I have seen several versions of this story (which, to me, confirms it as an urban myth), but the best one relates to an England cricket side that was touring Australia in the 1920s or 1930s. They were on their way to the kind of up-country match which, alas, no longer features so prominently in the highly professionalized world of modern international cricket, when their motor coach hit a kangaroo. The cricketers got out to inspect the damage and thought it would be great fun to have a team photograph which included the apparently dead kangaroo. They hoisted it to its feet and dressed it in an MCC blazer. As they were posing, the kangaroo, who was not dead but only stunned, came to and hopped off into the bush still wearing the yellow and red striped flannel. Versions of the story often include subsequent third-party sightings of a mob of kangaroos that includes one who is wearing a coat. In 2003 the film *Kangaroo Jack* used this device to drive a plot in which a kangaroo hops off into the outback wearing a coat stuffed with money belonging to New York gangsters.

Perhaps the archetypal version of the clothed kangaroo story is recorded in the hand-produced brochure *Souvenir of Coolamon, 1881–1934*, which was produced as part of the Back to Coolamon Week festivities in 1934:

Many jokes have been made about our late show secretary, Mr. J. H. Seymour, riding a kangaroo. It is quite true. On one occasion a number of the Stinson family, Mr. J. H. Seymour and some other visiting friends, were driving kangaroos into a special trap-yard. The girls at the station had made a red suit to be put on a big 'old man kangaroo'. We yarded a large number of kangaroos and slaughtered them with the exception of one extra big 'old man'. This one we lassooed and dressed him a full rig-out of coat, waistcoat and trousers. We had some fun for a time boxing with him, but all were chary about his hindlegs. Then J.H.S. said he would have a ride on him, so we got the big 'roo out of the yard and after some difficulty J.H.S. got on his back. Then he implored us not to let go the rope. So we ran along with it. It was very funny, and the girls screamed with laughter. After the ride we tied a strap round the kangaroo's neck with a bell attached and let him go. We raced after him on our horses till he got to a big mob of his mates who, of course, got for their lives with the 'roo with the red suit with jangling bell following. That was the last we saw of the red suit or bell.

This must have been in the early 1880s and shows (in addition to being the fullest variant of the clothed kangaroo story I have come across) just how casually people in the Australian countryside at that time treated the lives of kangaroos. But time and time again they are noted as destructive pests and for a settler society which was fearfully vulnerable to even slight variations in crop production or the availability of grazing, this view is not surprising.[12]

Kangaroos had also become part of the English diet by this time. Later editions of the famous *Mrs Beeton's Book of Household Management* gave a number of kangaroo recipes including the famous kangaroo steamer as well as pickled kangaroo tail and roast wallaby. On 9 November 1875 William Morris found himself at Kelmscott Manor and the servants, not having prepared the house properly for his arrival (had he remembered to tell them he was coming? Knowing Morris, probably not), he had to make do with a tin of kangaroo meat. In the twentieth century kangaroo meat was commonly used as a filler in tins of cat and dog food and only recently has it become a gourmet delicacy again. Indeed, in Australia until the 1980s and '90s, kangaroo meat was permitted only as a pet food and was not considered fit for human consumption at all.

In 1946 British wives of Australian servicemen found themselves unable to join their repatriated husbands because of an alleged shortage of ships going to Australia. They set up a vigorous protest under the umbrella name the Kangaroo Club which was, to them, the obvious way of designating their Australian affiliation.

In the 1960s Australia was in the grip of the 'populate or perish' policy and was encouraging migration from the UK in significant numbers. Many of the people who moved to Australia at this time benefitted from the Australian government's assisted passage scheme and became known, from the contribution that they had to make towards their fare, as the Ten Pound Poms. It can be no coincidence that this movement coincided with the rise to fame of the popular entertainer Rolf Harris, who offered a congenial and amusing vision of Australia. In 1960 his song 'Tie Me Kangaroo Down, Sport' spent some time riding high in the popular music charts and is still extremely familiar. Although the lyrics refer to all manner of Australian animals, it is to the kangaroo that Harris turned to brand his lyrics unmistakably Australian.

Kangaroos had reached the United States by the 1820s and were being exhibited in travelling menageries there. There have,

Rolf Harris with a kangaroo, *c.* late 1960s.

for many years, been alleged sightings of kangaroos across the US. There are two attested cases of escapees from zoos (both in 1968) and who knows how many individual kangaroo owners have tired of their pets (or their pets have tired of them) and released them into the wild. However, these individual cases (if there are any beyond the two cases we know of) could not account for the large number of kangaroo sightings that have been reported in the US since the nineteenth century, with a large cluster in the Chicago region and in Wisconsin in the 1970s. These sightings often have a mystical air since the kangaroo appears to manifest and dematerialize before it can be caught, although one Chicago sighting in 1974 allegedly involved two policemen who actually cornered what they clearly thought was a kangaroo and attempted to handcuff it. The kangaroo made off into the night and, if the policeman were to be believed, it can only have been an escapee from a zoo or circus – and yet no such escape was reported or noted at the time.

A very similar pattern of sightings has been reported in Japan on a regular basis since 2003. However, as a wallaby which escaped from a zoo in Ottawa, Canada, in 2008 shows, there may be a very slim relationship between the point of escape and the

Stereograph card photo of a kangaroo at the Philadelphia World's Fair of 1876.

point of sighting because this little creature was found dead over 80 kilometres from its place of incarceration. In July 2011 a wallaby called Tyson escaped from his home in Onoway, Alberta, and is still on the loose: his grandfather and father also escaped captivity and the father is still sighted regularly over a year after his getaway. The Gan Garoo Australia Park in northern Israel has a fine collection of kangaroos so we can be confident that, sooner or later, they will be colonizing the Golan Heights.

Whether the phantom kangaroo has simply made its way east or whether the growth of Internet Forteanism is the reason is hard to judge. There is, however, an attested feral population on Oahu in the state of Hawai'i. These animals descend from a male, a female and a joey bought from an Australian ship that visited Honolulu in 1916. The adults escaped following an attack by dogs (during which the joey was killed) and have survived ever since. The population has been as high as 250 but it may now be rather lower than that. The Kangaroo Conservation Center at Alpharetta, Georgia, has been in operation since 1984. It started with just two animals and now has the largest kangaroo collection outside Australia numbering some 300 individuals from as many as twelve different species. The centre also sells kangaroos to approved and vetted buyers; it currently has eastern and western greys and reds on offer, together with a bettong which will be free to the right facility.

The American kangaroo has also been associated with a legendary cryptozoological creature the chupacabra. In 1934 in Tennessee a rampaging chupacabra wreaked havoc on livestock and even tore an Alsatian dog to shreds. The chupacabra is said, in some versions, to be a marsupial carnivore and a descendant of the South American marsupials which are a common ancestor of the Australian kangaroo. Chupacabra shootings usually reveal mangy coyotes, but it is interesting to note how ready people are, even now, to use the kangaroo as the template for any bizarre animal. Indeed, a kangaroo was the vehicle of a notorious hoax. In 1909 and 1910 the US was in the grip of a frenzied interest in another cryptid creature, the so-called Jersey Devil. Philadelphia Zoo, only half seriously, offered a US$10,000 reward for its capture. Two pranksters called Norman Jefferies and Jacob Hope duly led a bizarre creature up to claim the prize. They claimed it was an Australian vampire bat, but it was, in fact, a kangaroo they had bought, painted with stripes and glued wings and claws onto. Again, when something weird is wanted, the kangaroo fits the bill.[13]

By the later nineteenth century kangaroos were becoming quite common in Britain and the famous wild animal dealer, Charles Jamrach, was selling them for £20 each. One man who was especially interested in them was the astonishing Frank Buckland. He was the son of William Buckland, dean of Christchurch, celebrated palaeontologist and a man who attempted to eat his way through the animal kingdom. Frank tried the same but, for

Caged kangaroos in Charles Jamrach's wild animal shop; from the *Illustrated London News* (1887).

him, gustatory experiment was more in the way of public good
than private sensation – he loved kangaroos and thought their
tails would offer a superior version of oxtail soup.

As well as being a naturalist and collector, Frank Buckland
was a leading light in the acclimatization movement that flour-
ished in the UK for about twenty years from the 1860s, but had
a longer life elsewhere.[14] This movement, which started as a mixture of serious scientific endeavour and a money-making scheme
in France, was global and had manifestations in Britain, Australia, New Zealand, Canada, the United States and Russia. The

movement became a large-scale scientific experiment and was designed to exploit the great animal wealth that the European empires were beginning to amass by domesticating those exotic animals on home territory and thus solving the problem of feeding a growing industrial working class that was culturally and physically separated from the source of food production. Kangaroos were just one of the animals that Buckland considered as a potentially large-scale stock animal in Britain (as were horses, but he admitted that even calling horse meat 'hippocrene' would not get the British to eat it), but he finally settled on elands as the most promising candidate and, although there were some serious attempts to farm them, the project never really took off. Although there were successful acclimatization projects around the world (for example, merino sheep in Australia and trout in New Zealand), nothing worked on any grand scale. In France the approach was more systematic and in 1857 the Société Zoologique d'Acclimatation offered a range of medals with worthwhile monetary prizes attached (between £20 and £80) for the successful acclimatization of a range of animals including the eastern and western grey kangaroos.[15]

In New Zealand a small colony of wallabies – specifically parma wallabies (*Macropus parma*) – still survives on Kawau Island. These are the legacy of Governor George Grey who, in the 1870s, introduced kangaroos, wallabies, antelope, deer, monkeys, zebra, peacocks, kookaburras and numerous other creatures (it must be remembered that New Zealand has no indigenous mammals). Few of these introductions thrived but the wallabies are still going strong. New Zealand is lucky that Grey's well-meaning attempts have largely failed because introduced mammals have destroyed indigenous flora and birdlife there, while across the Tasman it is almost a civic duty to kill at least one possum (a heavily protected animal in Australia) a year. This curious history has meant that New Zealand is perhaps the only country where green politics and environmental activism are closely aligned with the hunting and fishing lobbies. As mentioned in chapter One, these Kawau Island wallabies are now returning to re-stock their species' original mainland Australian range. The Auckland and North Canterbury Acclimatisation Societies established colonies of red-necked wallabies near Waimate in the 1860s and 1870s. These are now the object of extermination campaigns and populations also inhabit (perhaps that should be infest? I think that is what a New Zealander might say) other areas of New Zealand and, thanks to George Grey, the islands in the Hauraki Gulf. Interestingly – given their success in Great Britain – attempts to establish populations of kangaroos proper in New Zealand have been unsuccessful. The Southland Acclimatisation Society made several attempts to establish kangaroo colonies at Bluff Hill, but no group of kangaroos ever thrived there.[16]

Almost more than any other exotic animal, kangaroos appear to have been able to effect a diasporic transformation in the countries they have visited. Colonies live wild in various places but they are also, as we have seen in the cases of the United States and Japan, the subject of significant cryptozoological speculation. In 1855 the Devonshire seaside town of Budleigh Salterton was plagued by a mysterious visitation to the extent that the townspeople were scared to go out. Memories and legends of that London monster, Spring Heeled Jack, circulated and added to the terror of the inhabitants of this small community and others where mysterious footprints were found in the snow. There was a media frenzy about this and a good deal of often contrary speculation which makes it difficult to unravel what really happened. One account tells us that after three days the mysterious visitant was shot by a plucky farmer and proved to be a kangaroo.

Red-necked wallaby (*Macropus rufogriseus*).

But where did it come from? I have made an extensive study of the travelling menageries that criss-crossed nineteenth-century England and almost invariably included kangaroos among the itinerant rarities, but there was none in the vicinity of Budleigh Salterton at that time. There was a pair of kangaroos living in a private menagerie in nearby Exeter, but no report of any escape. My guess is that the kangaroo report is not actually true and derives from the speculation of a local clergyman. What is important, though, is that when a mysterious set of footprints appeared it did not take long before someone imagined that there was a kangaroo on the loose. As we have seen, it seems natural to explain almost any strange occurrence by means of a kangaroo.

Kangaroos – or rather wallabies – have been living wild in Britain for many years. The oldest established colony is to found on the island of Inconnachan in Loch Lomond which was established in the 1920s by Lady Arran Colquhoun and is still going strong in spite of a June 2009 decision by the managers of the estate to exterminate them on account of the damage they were allegedly doing to the island. A vigorous campaign, both local and national, appears to have saved them and wallabies were certainly still there in September 2010. The island supports a population of about 60 individual animals, the more intrepid of which occasionally swim to the mainland or hop across the ice during the harsher winters.

Another population is to be found in the Peak District of Derbyshire and this established itself in the 1940s following a successful break-out from a nearby zoo in Leek belonging to Captain Henry Courtney Brocklehurst. A yak also escaped but alas it was recaptured before it could find a partner and begin a

Feral red-necked wallaby (*Macropus rufogriseus*) in rural Derbyshire, UK.

truly exotic new population. Again, patience will result in a wallaby sighting in this area of the northern Midlands and, it is reported, further south into Staffordshire. Wallaby sightings have also been confirmed on the Lincolnshire–Norfolk border and it is not beyond the realms of possibility that these derive from a travelling group from Derbyshire. The notoriously harsh winter of 1963 greatly reduced the colony's numbers but the species *Macropus rufogriseus banksiana* is used to harsh and cold conditions in its Australian mainland and Tasmanian range and so enough survived to re-establish viable numbers. In 2001 *The Sun* newspaper reported that eastern European immigrants (one of the many targets for moral panic in the British media at the time) were capturing the wallabies and killing them for their meat.

Another colony is to be found in Ashdown Forest in Sussex. This is a very interesting one since Ashdown Forest is the location of A. A. Milne's Winnie the Pooh stories and so it is apt that the home of the fictional Kanga and her joey Roo should now be hosting some genuine marsupial visitors. A large colony also lives on the Isle of Man and, again, these derive from an escape from the local Curraghs Wildlife Park. Wallabies have been found on the islands of Bute and Lundy and in the 1980s Dublin Zoo dealt with an explosion in its wallaby population by shipping the surplus animals off to the island of Lambay where, I understand, they have settled down happily.

A population of semi-wild wallabies lived at Whipsnade Zoo from the 1930s onwards, but numbers have greatly fallen, largely due to very hard winters, from a high point of 900 animals in 1978. At Marwell Zoo, just outside Winchester in Hampshire, a semi-wild colony lives in what used to be called Wallaby Wood – it is now more formally designated the Australian Bush Walk – and visitors can note the impact of genetic selection by the presence of so many little white heads peering from pouches. These are the offspring of the alpha male Snow King. Penshurst Vineyard (near Tunbridge Wells in Kent and not to be confused with Penshurst Vineyard in Victoria) used to have a mob of wallabies hopping round the vines and these featured, for a time, on the labels of the excellent Kentish wine that is made there. One colony that is definitely extinct is the one that was established on the tiny Channel Island of Herm. These were all eaten by soldiers stationed there during the First World War.

The strangeness of the macropod is borne out by recent trends in the UK. Mary Davies has been breeding wallabies on her estate in West Sussex for ten years and uses them to keep the grass down on her extensive lawns.[17] In 2009 the exotic animal dealership Waveney Wildlife was selling wallabies for £800 for a male and female pair and reported that they were having trouble keeping up with the demand for them from people who, like Ms Davies, want to use them as interesting and exotic lawn mowers. Waveney claim that a fence at least 5 feet in height is required to keep the animals secure, but I am doubtful that this is sufficient and, indeed, in June 2010 traffic on the M55 near the holiday resort of Blackpool was brought to a standstill while local police and a vet from the nearby wildlife park attempted to capture an errant wallaby. This was privately owned (presumably by someone without a 5-foot fence) and so there is every reason to believe, should the trend take hold, that there will be more wallaby colonies living wild in England in the near future.

Wallabies lived in Prussia in the late nineteenth century, again as a deliberately introduced population. Between 1887 and 1893 the original two males and three females grew to form a small colony of some 40 animals. However, following the death of their keeper, by 1895 they had been hunted to extinction. Near Bonn a colony of 70 wallabies was introduced in the first decade of the twentieth century but it did not survive the war as a viable entity and the survivors were all moved to zoos. There was also a colony outside Hamburg. Short-lived wallaby colonies were also to be found in the former Czechoslovakia (Prague), Hungary (Szenna), Poland (Krobielowice) and the Ukraine (Askania-Nova). A significant colony is still to be found in Émancé in the Rambouillet Forest just south of Paris. These are escapees from a local zoo but have established themselves very well and are much loved by the local people, who have developed a tourist trade – and a thriving

Albino wallaby
at Amnéville zoo,
France.

business in insurance claims for wallaby-related car accidents
– based on their exotic guests. Kangaroos have also been seen
in the Netherlands. In Austria, a kangaroo that escaped from a
German zoo in 2007 was last seen in 2010, while another called
Sumsi is still on the hop, near the village of Preding. However, in
spite of the fact that there are kangaroos living wild in Austria it
is possible to buy t-shirts and other tourist memorabilia pro-
claiming that 'there are no kangaroos in Austria'. This is allegedly

a reaction against the potential confusion of Austria with Australia (and there is a joke that George W. Bush once said, while contemplating a visit to Austria, that he was looking forward to seeing some kangaroos), but given the tendency of Austrian domestic politics to xenophobia one cannot help feeling that something more sinister is at work.

When the kangaroo is abroad it appears simultaneously to be a manifestation of the strange and the marvellous, but it can also be a surprisingly reassuring and familiar presence, especially in Britain. It remains a bearer of strangeness but is also strangely at home in foreign countries and is quite literally now at home in many.

5 Tailpiece: The Curious Kangaroo

The people who buy purses or bottle-openers made from kangaroo scrotums or lethal back-scratchers made from kangaroo
paws from the souvenir shops around Sydney Harbour's Circular
Quay or, indeed, those who buy the more tasteful wallets, hand-
bags (sometimes with the fur still on), briefcases and belts made
from the super-soft but durable leather of the kangaroo – and
even David Beckham whose football boots are custom-made for
him from kangaroo leather – are participating in the paradox
that marks the animal as peculiarly loaded with meaning. It is an
icon and a pest. It is loveable and scary. When Australians were
polled a decade ago about whether they would feel comfortable
having native animals living in their neighbourhoods, many
were very comfortable with koalas but only a minority said they
would like kangaroos hopping about. And yet practically every
Australian would identify his or her country first and foremost
with the kangaroo.

A further puzzle centres on the origin of kangaroos since
there are, apparently, no transitional fossils which take us from
the earliest proto-marsupials to the modern-day kangaroo. This
has been used as the cornerstone of the creationist argument
against evolution – as creationist publications admit, kangaroos
are often used as the example to test the creationist belief, which

Kangaroo Tobacco packaging, c. 1900.

is summed up in this typical passage from one of many creationist websites:

> Evolutionists explain the wide variety of kangaroos and their specialized survival methods as millions of years of trial and effort, chance mutation and selection. However, kangaroos' superb design, their sophisticated reproductive

Australia Day poster, *Kangaroo Study no. 7* by Joseph McGlennon, 2010.

methods and their amazing, energy-efficient locomotion did not come by any evolutionary process. For example, unless the pouch and the joey's ability to find it were fully functional, they would have left no offspring.

Kangaroos are ingenious examples of God's craftsmanship, designed by a Creator who knew perfectly what He was doing. To Him all praise, glory and honor is forever due.

In 1834 the English poet John Abraham Heraud was also meditating on this matter as he was planning his didactic epic *The Judgement of the Flood*, which did for verse what John Martin did for painting. Heraud had no hesitation in situating kangaroos on the gangplank leading up to the Ark:

> The Kangaroo, on its hind legs sustained,
> And moving fast, high bounding and afar,
> Its fore too brief, and but as hands employed
> To dig with, or to feed.

Twenty-five years later Charles Darwin used kangaroos to illustrate a point about species affinity in *On The Origin of Species* and this may show that he was mindful of the animal's somewhat anomalous position and felt it necessary to ensure that his controversial book at least mentioned it, although he did not dwell on the kangaroo in any detail. He had seen rat-kangaroos on his visit to Australia on the *Beagle* in 1836 – surprisingly, he did not see any kangaroos proper although he visited places where they lived in abundance – and found them (as well as the platypus) so unusual that he noted:

> An unbeliever in every thing beyond his own reason might exclaim, 'Surely two distinct creators must have been at work; their object, however, has been the same, and certainly the end in each case is complete.'

Currently, kangaroo evolution is being used as a tool for understanding the climate of early Australia and how and at what rate it changed. For example, kangaroo dentition shows adaptation which can be used to reconstruct the historic flora and thus model the climactic conditions that would have enabled the specific plants to grow in the relevant areas.

In 1933 the Australian national poet A. B. 'Banjo' Paterson found no difficulties in entitling his book of children's verse *The*

Animals that Noah Forgot. Kangaroos make several appearances in the charming collection, often as somewhat irascible characters, but their most sustained appearance is to be found in his poem 'Fur and Feathers':

The emus formed a football team
Up Walgett way;
Their dark-brown sweaters were a dream
But kangaroos would sit and scream
To watch them play.

'Now, butterfingers,' they would call,
And such-like names;
The emus couldn't hold the ball
– They had no hands – but hands aren't all
In football games.

A match against the kangaroos
They played one day.
The kangaroos were forced to choose
Some wallabies and wallaroos
That played in grey.

The rules that in the West prevail
Would shock the town;
For when a kangaroo set sail
An emu jumped upon his tail
And fetched him down.

A whistler duck as referee
Was not admired.
He whistled so incessantly

The teams rebelled, and up a tree
He soon retired.

The old marsupial captain said,
'It's do or die!'
So down the ground like fire he fled
And leaped above an emu's head
And scored a try.

Then shouting, 'Keep it on the toes!'
The emus came.
Fierce as the flooded Bogan flows
They laid their foemen out in rows
And saved the game.

On native pear and Darling pea
They dined that night:
But one man was an absentee:
The whistler duck – their referee –
Had taken flight.

The cover of the first edition has a splendid illustration by Norman Lindsay showing an emu jumping on a football-carrying kangaroo's tail while a kookaburra laughs from the branches of an adjacent gum tree.

Another oddity is that the phrase 'kangaroo court' appears to derive not from Australia but from the California Gold Rush where its first use is recorded. There have been various stabs at understanding its origin. One explanation is that such courts usually dealt with people digging on other people's patches – 'claim jumpers'. Another – and I like this one – says that the vacant stares of the jury in these informal courts made them look

A 'kangaroo court' in progress on board the USS *Seattle* in the early 1910s.

like kangaroos. Perhaps the most likely hazards the guess that such courts jumped from point to point and then swiftly to a verdict. But that the phrase is not Australian seems another piece of kangaroo curiosity.

The curiosity provoked by the kangaroo has also been encapsulated in a conundrum known as the 'kangaroo paradox'. This is the phenomenon – which many readers will have noticed – by which, having become aware of a word, you suddenly start hearing it everywhere. It is so named because in the first experiment on the phenomenon people were asked how many times they had heard the word 'kangaroo' in the previous week and were then asked again a week later. The number of hearings increased dramatically in the second week with some people actually mishearing other words as 'kangaroo'. It seems to me somehow apt that a process which involves commonly seeing (or hearing) something that you thought was rare should be named for the kangaroo and that the process itself should be deemed a paradox.

To write about kangaroos is always to write about curiosity and paradox. It is not possible to write about kangaroos without writing about Australia, or even to see a kangaroo or a picture of a kangaroo without thinking about Australia, so closely are the country and the animal connected. Perhaps no other animal is quite so closely identified with a country and a culture. While one does associate elephants with Thailand, tigers with India and pandas with China, these are not connections of quite the same order. Most Chinese people never see a panda and Indians avoid tigers if they possibly can; Thais do see elephants but they see them as working animals. The bear may be almost as closely identified with Russia, but that identification is on a wholly symbolic level and has little, if anything, to do with the day-to-day

Matschie's tree-kangaroo (*Dendrolagus matschiei*).

Kangaroo sculptures, Perth, 2007.

interactions of Russians and bears. Australians, however, do interact with wild kangaroos on a regular basis. You do not have to venture far from the urban centres to encounter kangaroos, and all the major cities have zoos and wildlife parks where kangaroos can be seen. In Sydney there are at least three such facilities and every day you can see Australians looking at the kangaroos and the kangaroos looking at the Australians. And had you been in Sydney in 1850 you could have seen the same thing in the grounds of the Sir Joseph Banks Hotel in Botany Bay where there was a small menagerie of Australian animals.[1]

And yet, writing about kangaroos from within Australia con-stitutes a constant questioning. Why are these common animals not better understood? Why do Australians have such difficulty with the idea of eating kangaroo meat? What is the truth about kangaroo culling? How did a creature widely perceived as a ser-ious agricultural menace and as a threat to the economy become the national symbol? Why is the kangaroo so strange?

The kangaroo, in the enforced paradoxes of its nature, remains suspended in this web of questions. And yet, in spite of its unique-ness, if the kangaroo did not exist we would have to invent it, for how else could the burden of strangeness be carried for us?

This book started with a discussion of the kangaroo as a sig-nifier of a change in the world order as deployed in the TV programme *FlashForward*. In the eighteenth and early nineteenth centuries the settlement of Australia also heralded a change in the world order. A new mindset was suddenly required to take into account a very real change in the geographical order of the world (Australia, New Zealand and dozens of Pacific Islands had been added and the Great Southern Continent had been sub-tracted), as well as in zoological classification systems and the way in which people thought about the natural world. And the kangaroo somehow came to symbolize all that.

Today, the kangaroo represents a further change, one that goes beyond the master metaphor of strangeness. Increasingly, the kangaroo is used to signify the fragile landscapes and ecosystems of Australia which will, I suspect, be one of the living laboratories in which the realities of climate change, caused by humans or not, will be tested. In this sense the kangaroo remains a signifier of change as the technological exploration and reassessment that climate change demands seems every bit as much a voyage into the unknown as were the voyages of the early European explorers. The discoveries that may result are, potentially, every bit as revolutionary as the realization that there were kangaroos in the world.

Timeline of the Kangaroo

60,000–50,000 BCE	50,000 BCE	14,000 BCE	6,000 BCE
First human settlement of Australia	Pre-Estuarine rock art includes first images of kangaroos	Extinction of megafauna	Estuarine rock art includes first 'X-ray' drawings of kangaroos

1699	1711	1770–73	1780s
British expedition under Dampier explores Western Australian coastline	First undisputed European image of a kangaroo in Cornelis de Bruijn's *Reizen over Moskovie, door Persie en Indie*	1770 sees the first sighting of a kangaroo by Sir Joseph Banks from on board Captain Cook's *Endeavour*; in 1773 Joseph Stubbs completes his kangaroo painting	French exploration of Western Australian coastline; the First Fleet arrives in Botany Bay in 1788

1877–80	1891–2	1895–9	1908
Queensland passes its Marsupial Destruction Act in 1877; New South Wales proposes the Marsupials Destruction Bill in 1879, and in 1880 passes the Pastures and Stock Protection Act	Olivia Mayne wins test case over boxing kangaroo proving a married woman's right to enter into a contract in 1891; boxing kangaroo exhibited at the Royal Aquarium, London, the following year	The silent film *Das Boxende Känguruh* is screened in Germany in 1895; *Dot and the Kangaroo* by Ethel C. Pedley is published in 1899	Inclusion of the kangaroo on the official coat of arms of Australia

| 100 CE | 500 | 1593 | 1629 |

Contacts begin between China, Indonesia, the Middle East, the Mediterranean and Australia

Freshwater rock art includes 'decorative X-ray' images of kangaroos

Possibly the first European image of a kangaroo, in *Speculum orbis terrae*

Dutch expedition under Pelsaert sights tammar wallaby, the first confirmed European encounter with a kangaroo species

| 1789–93 | 1804 | 1820s | 1845–63 |

Live kangaroos arrive in Britain and France in 1789. In 1790–91 live kangaroos are exhibited in Scotland and London, and by 1793 kangaroos are living and breeding in Windsor Great Park

French expedition under Baudin returns to France with live kangaroos; Australian garden set up at Malmaison

Kangaroos exhibited in the US; in 1826 a Dutch expedition collects tree-kangaroos, previously unknown to Europeans, from New Guinea

Publication of John Gould's *The Mammals of Australia*

| 1934 | 1966 | 1988 | 2009 |

New South Wales passes Pastures Protection Act offering some protection to kangaroos for the first time

First screening of *Skippy*

Publication of Australian federal g overnment report on the kangaroo industry

THINKK established as a kangaroo research centre in Sydney

References

1 WHAT IS A KANGAROO?

1 Emily Dickinson, letter to Thomas Higginson, July 1862.
2 To learn more about the taxonomy, physiology and behaviour of
  macropods, their discovery by Europeans and the palaeontological
  record, see D. Clode, *Continent of Curiosities* (Port Melbourne, 2006);
  D. Clode, *Prehistoric Giants: The Megafauna of Australia* (Melbourne,
  2009); C. M. Finney, *To Sail beyond the Sunset* (Adelaide, 1984);
  T. Flannery, *Country* (Melbourne, 2004); S. Jackson and K. Vernes,
  Kangaroo: Portrait of an Extraordinary Marsupial (Sydney, 2010);
  C. Johnson, *Australia's Mammal Extinctions* (Cambridge, 2006);
  P. Olsen, *Upside Down World* (Canberra, 2010); and I. Parsonson,
  The Australian Ark (Collingwood, 2000).
3 W. R. Telfer and M. J. Garde, 'Indigenous Knowledge of Rock
  Kangaroo Ecology in Western Arnhem Land', *Human Ecology*,
  XXXIV (2006), pp. 379–406.
4 Bridie Smith, 'Kangaroo Clue to Skin Cancer', *The Age* (1
  December 2009), at www.theage.com.au, accessed 12 July 2012.
5 For more about the *Batavia* massacre, see M. Dash, *Batavia's
  Graveyard* (London, 2003), and P. FitzSimons, *Batavia* (Sydney,
  2011).
6 T. Flannery, *The Future Eaters: An Ecological History of the Australasian Lands and Peoples* (Sydney, 1994). J. Auty, 'Red Plague, Grey
  Plague: The Kangaroo Myths and Legends', *Australian Mammalogy*,
  XXVI (2004), pp. 33–6, offers a comprehensive review of historic
  kangaroo population numbers including a critique of Flannery.

7 E. Rolls, *They All Ran Wild* (Sydney, 1984).

8 G. Grigg, 'Kangaroo Harvesting and the Conservation of the Sheep Rangelands', *Australian Zoologist*, XXIV (1988), pp. 124–8.

9 This report has formed the basis for most subsequent thinking on the conservation of kangaroos and the development of the kangaroo industry. It would be true to say that the debate on both issues is still remarkably polarized and that conservationists, ecologists and agriculturalists have few points of common ground.

10 THINKK, *A Shot in the Dark: A Report on Kangaroo Harvesting* (Sydney, 2009); THINKK, *Shooting our Wildlife: An Analysis of the Law and Policy Governing the Killing of Kangaroos* (Sydney, 2010); THINKK, *Advocating Kangaroo Meat: Towards Ecological Benefit or Plunder?* (Sydney, 2010).

11 Sanna Trad, 'Furore over Canberra Kangaroo Cull', *The Australian* (20 May 2008), at www.theaustralian.com.au, accessed 12 July 2012.

12 For a full discussion on the kangaroo naming controversy, see R.M.W. Dixon, *The Languages of Australia* (Cambridge, 1980).

2 THE KANGAROO MEETS ITS NEW NEIGHBOURS

1 Some readers may feel that this section on Indigenous culture is rather brief. While this is true, it is not because of any disrespect to Indigenous culture but rather the opposite. This book is written in an Australian context and it is wiser to let Indigenous people speak for themselves on these matters than to speculate, perhaps erroneously, on what their opinions or cultural beliefs might be. The section on Marlu is based on Kado Muir's intervention in C. Dickman and R. Woodford Ganf, *A Fragile Balance* (Fisherman's Bend, 2007). R. Kenny, *The Lamb Enters the Dreaming* (Carlton North, 2007), offers a brilliant analysis of the impact of settler culture and agriculture on the Wotjobaluk people of Victoria in the mid-nineteenth century and the complex interactions between people, animals and country.

2 R. Layton, *Australian Rock Art: A New Synthesis* (Cambridge, 2010), is a comprehensive introduction to this art form.

3 There are many books on the art of Indigenous Australia but
  G. Bardon, *Papunya: A Place Made after the Story* (Melbourne,
  2004), probably offers the best starting point. M. Pickering et al.,
  Yiwarra Kuju (Canberra, 2010), contains a sustained account of
  the Dreamtime in relation to contemporary Indigenous Australian
  art, while Wally Caruana's analysis of the great Clifford Possum
  Tjapaltjarri's 1972 painting *Bushfire II* in F. Cubillo and W.
  Caruana, eds, *Aboriginal and Torres Strait Islander Art* (Canberra,
  2010), gives a concise and sensitive explanation of the problems
  faced by Indigenous painters in approaching the depiction of
  traditional material and also the way in which the characteristic
  dots of desert painting could be used to obscure sensitive parts
  of the image.

It should be remembered that traditional material culture
did not include formal painting except as seen in rock art, ritual
sand design and the decorative work on wooden shields and the
like. Indeed, Indigenous Australian material culture has never
been extensive because the main creative work has always been
the elaboration and maintenance of the Dreamtime. So the work
done at Bardon's studios essentially refocused traditional modes
of representation by using Western materials and a Western
approach to exhibiting. The artists who worked at Papunya
familiarized the world with the 'dot-painting' style, which is
perhaps the most instantly recognizable kind of Indigenous
Australian painting, but there are other kinds, notably the large
colour field ochre paintings of the Kimberley artists and the
detailed figurative and graphic work done in the Tiwi and
Torres Straits Islands.

Previously, Indigenous artists had largely followed Western
models and the most famous of these was Albert Namatjira,
whose distinctive desert landscapes offered the rest of Australia
the realization that the Indigenous people were capable of
immense creativity and had talent to offer. Namatjira collected
many honours and was the first Indigenous Australian to be
made an Australian citizen, in 1957. Because he had married

into a forbidden kinship group he spent much of his life ostracized by his own, the Arrernte people. After the granting of his citizenship Namatjira was allowed to vote, to own property and to drink alcohol but, as an Arrernte man, he was constrained to share everything with his extended family and this included alcohol, which was forbidden to Indigenous Australians. As a result Namatjira found himself sentenced to six months with labour. This destroyed his health and he died in 1959 shortly after his early release from prison. On Namatjira, see Nadine Amadio's very accessible monograph *Albert Namatjira: The Life and Work of an Australian Painter* (South Melbourne, 1986).

4 See R. M. Younger, *Kangaroo Images through the Ages* (Hawthorn, 1988). The Spanish and Portuguese voyages are dealt with very fully in M. Estensen, *Terra Australis Incognita: The Spanish Quest for the Mysterious Great South Land* (Crow's Nest, 2006), and W. Eisler, *Terra Australis: The Furthest Shore* (Cambridge, 1995).

5 See J. Bonnemans, E. Forsyth and B. Smith, eds, *Baudin in Australian Waters* (Melbourne, 1988); P. Carter and S. Hunt, *Terre Napoléon: Australia through French Eyes, 1800–1804* (Sydney, 1999); D. Clode, *Voyages to the South Seas: In Search of Terres Australes* (Melbourne 2007); L. R. Marchant, *France Australe* (Perth, 1982); and P. Godard, *1772: The French Annexation of New Holland* (Perth, 2009), for accounts of the French involvement in Australia.

There are many theories as to who the first non-Indigenous people to 'discover' Australia were. Cases have been made for the Egyptians, Phoenicians and the Maya as well as the Greeks, Romans, Arabs and Chinese. Certainly writers of the classical period speak of a southern continent but it is often unclear whether they are speaking of something they know about or following a specific preconception of geography. Pomponius Mela left a map which shows something that looks Australia-like, while in *A Traveller's True Tale* – a fantasy that might qualify as the first work of science fiction – Lucian of Samosata does mention a southern land where there are animals that carry their young in pouches. D. Haveric, *Australia in Muslim Discovery* (Geelong, 2006), offers a comprehensive overview of the case for the Arabs and Chinese.

Clearly, it is unlikely that a definitive answer to this question will ever be forthcoming but it seems to me very possible that people from the ancient Mediterranean could have known about Australia and might even have visited it. There are two reasons for this. The first is that they knew and traded with Asian peoples who were certainly coming to Australia by what in Europe was known as the Middle Ages and may have been coming earlier. The second is that it is often forgotten that you do not have to make a large-scale open sea crossing to reach Australia from Europe – it can almost all be done by using the coast-hugging methods that were the norm in the ancient world. The only reason that the western European explorers of the Enlightenment made such long voyages across open water – and especially across the Pacific – was that they were looking for things. They did not need to take such risks merely to reach Australia.

6 This painting was last seen at the Royal Society of Victoria.

7 On Banks, see P. O'Connor, *Joseph Banks* (London, 1987); on Hunter, see W. Moore, *The Knife Man* (London, 2005). J. Uglow, *The Lunar Men* (London, 2002), offers a remarkably readable and engaging account of the scientific culture in which men like Banks and Hunter were involved and, more generally, of the fad for science in eighteenth-century Britain.

8 See J. Blunden, ed., *Curious Colony* (Newcastle, 2010), and E. Ellis, *Rare and Curious* (Carlton, 2010), for accounts of early convict artists and, particularly, the Dixson and Macquarie chests.

9 I. Tree, *The Bird Man* (London, 1991), is the best introduction to Gould's life. See also D. Clode, *Continent of Curiosities* (Port Melbourne, 2006); P. Olsen, *Upside Down World* (Canberra, 2010); and R. Russell, *The Business of Nature: John Gould and Australia* (Canberra, 2011).

10 See J. Hamilton, *Napoleon, the Empress and the Artist* (East
   Roseville, 1999), and Carter and Hunt, *Terre Napoléon*.
11 See O'Connor, *Joseph Banks*.

3 THE KANGAROO AT HOME

 1 J. O'Connor, *Bottersnikes and Other Lost Things* (Carlton, 2009),
   offers a comprehensive survey of Australian children's literature
   including many examples of illustrations from these books showing
   kangaroos and other Australian wildlife.
 2 See B. Hatton and L. Thompson, 'Kangaroo', in M. Harper
   and R. White, eds, *Symbols of Australia* (Sydney, 2010),
   pp. 13–32.
 3 R. Perry, *Monash: The Outsider Who Won the War* (Sydney, 2004).
 4 After the war Josephine found her way back to Australia and
   is now in the museum at the Australian War Memorial. She is
   pictured in Department of Veterans' Affairs, *M is for Mates:
   Animals in Wartime from Ajax to Zep* (Canberra, 2009), which
   is a fascinating little book aimed primarily at children.
 5 A. Burt, ed., *The Colonial Cookbook* (Dee Why West, 1970), is largely
   a reprint of Abbott's book. M. Symons, *One Continuous Picnic* [1982]
   (revd edn, Melbourne, 2007) offers a comprehensive account of
   Australian gastronomy including consideration of kangaroo eating.
 6 Jasmin Afianos, 'Randy Roo Stalking Aussie Women', *Northern
   Territory News* (14 May 2010), at www.news.com.au, accessed
   14 February 2012.
 7 Ibid.
 8 Daniel Bourchier, 'Horny Roo Strikes Again', *Northern Territory News*
   (4 August 2010), at www.ntnews.com.au, accessed 12 July 2012.
 9 Brooke Baskin, 'Boxing Kangaroo Turns on Phyllis Johnson at
   Charleville', *The Courier-Mail* (26 July 2011), at www.couriermail.
   com.au, accessed 12 July 2012.
10 'Kangaroo Left in Cage on LA Street in Tourism Australia "G'Day
   USA" Campaign', *The Telegraph* (25 March 2010), at www.telegraph.
   co.uk, accessed 12 July 2012.

11 'Tourism Australia Accused over Caged Kangaroo Stunt', *Daily Telegraph* (25 March 2010), at www.news.com.au, accessed 14 February 2012.

12 J. Cheeseman et al., *Australian Accent* (Mosman, 2010), is a catalogue of an excellent exhibition of these fabrics and ceramics held at Mosman Art Gallery.

4 THE KANGAROO ABROAD

1 Henri Paget, 'Caged Kangaroo brought to Google Party', ninemsn (23 April 2010), at www.ninemsn.com.au, accessed 9 July 2012.

2 See M. Morton, ed., *Oudry's Painted Menagerie* (Los Angeles, 2007).

3 See H. Ritvo, *The Platypus and the Mermaid* (Cambridge, MA, 1997), and D. Clode, *Continent of Curiosities* (Port Melbourne, 2006).

4 See F. Fraser, *Princesses* (London, 2004). These kangaroos eventually found their way to the Australian garden at Malmaison.

5 J. Simons, *Rossetti's Wombat* (London, 2008), deals in some detail with Prince Alfred's visit to Australia and the exotic animal trade in Victorian England.

6 See J. Johnson and M. Anderson, *Australia Imagined* (Crawley, 2005).

7 See J. Allen, *Samuel Johnson's Menagerie* (Norwich, 2002).

8 M. Rothschild and Walter Rothschild, *The Man, the Museum, the Menagerie* (London, 2008).

9 G. Morey, *The Lincoln Kangaroos* (London, 1962).

10 Rosita Boland, 'Making Party Animal of a "Kangaroo"', *Irish Times* (10 October 2010), available at www.irishtimes.com, accessed 4 February 2012.

11 See H. Golder and D. Kirkby, 'Mrs Mayne and her Boxing Kangaroo: A Married Woman Tests her Property Rights in Colonial New South Wales', *Law and History Review*, XXI (2003), pp. 585–605. I am indebted to Nancy Cushing and Kevin Markwell for giving me access to their ongoing and still unpublished research into boxing kangaroos, especially in Australia.

12 I am indebted to Bill Stinson for alerting me to this local history material and giving me copies from his own collection.

13 See L. Coleman, *Mysterious America* (Winchester, MA, 1983), for a summary of cryptozoological occurrences of kangaroos and related creatures (real and imagined) in the United States.

14 On Frank Buckland, see J.H.O. Burgess, *The Curious World of Frank Buckland* (London, 1967), and J. Simons, *Rossetti's Wombat* (London, 2008); on William Buckland, see D. Cadbury, *The Dinosaur Hunters* (London, 2000).

15 See C. Lever, *They Dined on Eland* (London, 1992), for a very full account of acclimatization societies around the world.

16 See P. M. McDowall, *Gamekeepers for the Nation* (Canterbury, NZ, 1994).

17 David Wilkes, 'For Sale: The Wallabies Who Wannabe Lawn-mowers and will Keep your Grass Trim all Summer Long', Mail Online (13 May 2010), at www.mailonline.com, accessed 9 July 2012.

5 TAILPIECE: THE CURIOUS KANGAROO

1 M. St Leon, *Circus: The Australian Story* (Melbourne, 2011), has an illustration of these gardens showing, among other things, a man and a kangaroo looking at each other from different sides of a fence.

Select Bibliography

Allen, J., *Samuel Johnson's Menagerie* (Norwich, 2002)

Auty, J., 'Red Plague, Grey Plague: The Kangaroo Myths and Legends', *Australian Mammalogy*, XXVI (2004), pp. 33–6

Bardon, G., *Papunya: A Place Made after the Story* (Melbourne, 2004)

Blunden, J., ed., *Curious Colony* (Newcastle, 2010)

Bonnemans, J., E. Forsyth and B. Smith, eds, *Baudin in Australian Waters* (Melbourne, 1988)

Burgess, J.H.O., *The Curious World of Frank Buckland* (London, 1967)

Burt, A., ed., *The Colonial Cookbook* (Dee Why West, 1970)

Cadbury, D., *The Dinosaur Hunters* (London, 2000)

Carter, P., and S. Hunt, *Terre Napoléon: Australia through French Eyes, 1800–1804* (Sydney, 1999)

Cheeseman, J., et al., *Australian Accent* (Mosman, 2010)

Clode, D., *Continent of Curiosities* (Port Melbourne, 2006)

—, *Voyages to the South Seas: In Search of Terres Australes* (Melbourne, 2007)

—, *Prehistoric Giants: The Megafauna of Australia* (Melbourne, 2009)

Coleman, L., *Mysterious America* (Winchester, MA, 1983)

Cubillo, F., and W. Caruana, eds, *Aboriginal and Torres Strait Islander Art* (Canberra, 2010)

Dash, M., *Batavia's Graveyard* (London, 2003)

Department of Veterans' Affairs, *M is for Mates: Animals in Wartime from Ajax to Zep* (Canberra, 2009)

Dickman, C., and R. Woodford Ganf, *A Fragile Balance* (Fisherman's Bend, 2007)

Dixon, R.M.W., *The Languages of Australia* (Cambridge, 1980)

Eisler, W., *Terra Australis: The Furthest Shore* (Cambridge, 1995)

Ellis, E., *Rare and Curious* (Carlton, 2010)

Estensen, M., *Terra Australis Incognita: The Spanish Quest for the Mysterious Great South Land* (Crow's Nest, 2006)

Finney, C. M., *To Sail Beyond the Sunset* (Adelaide, 1984)

FitzSimons, P., *Batavia* (Sydney, 2011)

Flannery, T., *The Future Eaters: An Ecological History of the Australasian Lands and Peoples* (Sydney, 1994)

—, *Country* (Melbourne, 2004)

Fraser, F., *Princesses* (London, 2004)

Godard, P., *1772: The French Annexation of New Holland* (Perth, 2009)

Golder, H., and D. Kirkby, 'Mrs Mayne and her Boxing Kangaroo: A Married Woman Tests her Property Rights in Colonial New South Wales', *Law and History Review*, XXI (2003), pp. 585–605

Gould, J., *Gould's Mammals* (Newton Abbot, Devon, 1977)

—, with modern commentaries by J. M. Dixon, *Kangaroos* (North Sydney, 1973)

Grigg, G., 'Kangaroo Harvesting and the Conservation of the Sheep Rangelands', *Australian Zoologist*, XXIV (1988), pp. 124–8

Hahn, D., *The Tower Menagerie* (London, 2003)

Hamilton, J., *Napoleon, the Empress and the Artist* (East Roseville, 1999)

Harper, M., and M. White, *Symbols of Australia* (Sydney and Canberra, 2010)

Hatton, B., and L. Thompson, 'Kangaroo', in M. Harper and R. White, eds, *Symbols of Australia* (Sydney, 2010), pp. 13–32

Haveric, D., *Australia in Muslim Discovery* (Geelong, 2006)

Jackson, S., and K. Vernes, *Kangaroo: Portrait of an Extraordinary Marsupial* (Sydney, 2010)

Johnson, C., *Australia's Mammal Extinctions* (Cambridge, 2006)

Johnson, J., and M. Anderson, *Australia Imagined* (Crawley, 2005)

Kenny, R., *The Lamb Enters the Dreaming* (Carlton North, 2007)

Lever, C., *They Dined on Eland* (London, 1992)

McDowall, P. M., *Gamekeepers for the Nation* (Canterbury, 1994)

Marchant, L. R., *France Australe* (Perth, 1982)

Moore, W., *The Knife Man* (London, 2005)

Morey, G., *The Lincoln Kangaroos* (London, 1962)

Morton, M., ed., *Oudry's Painted Menagerie* (Los Angeles, 2007)

O'Connor, J., *Bottersnikes and Other Lost Things* (Carlton, 2009)

O'Connor, P., *Joseph Banks* (London, 1987)

Olsen, P., *Upside Down World* (Canberra, 2010)

Parsonson, I., *The Australian Ark* (Collingwood, 2000)

Perry, R., *Monash: The Outsider Who Won the War* (Sydney, 2004)

Pickering, M., et al., *Yiwarra Kuju* (Canberra, 2010)

Ritvo, H., *The Platypus and the Mermaid* (Cambridge, MA, 1997)

Rolls, E., *They All Ran Wild* (Sydney, 1984)

Rothschild, M., *Walter Rothschild: The Man, the Museum, the Menagerie* (London, 2008)

Russell, R., *The Business of Nature: John Gould and Australia* (Canberra, 2011)

St Leon, M., *Circus, The Australian Story* (Melbourne, 2011)

Simons, J., *Rossetti's Wombat* (London, 2008)

Symons, M., *One Continuous Picnic* [1982] (revd edn, Melbourne, 2007)

Telfer, W. R., and M. J. Garde, 'Indigenous Knowledge of Rock Kangaroo Ecology in Western Arnhem Land', *Human Ecology*, XXXIV (2006), pp. 379–406

THINKK, *A Shot in the Dark: A Report on Kangaroo Harvesting* (Sydney, 2009)

—, *Shooting our Wildlife: An Analysis of the Law and Policy Governing the Killing of Kangaroos* (Sydney, 2010)

—, *Advocating Kangaroo Meat: Towards Ecological Benefit or Plunder?* (Sydney, 2010)

Tree, I., *The Bird Man* (London, 1991)

Uglow, J., *The Lunar Men* (London, 2002)

Way, T., *A Crocodile in the Fernery* (Cirencester, 2008)

Younger, R. M., *Kangaroo Images through the Ages* (Hawthorn, 1988)

Associations and Websites

Most websites belonging to kangaroo-oriented organizations are devoted to conservation, protection and opposition to culling. The main ones are given below. These are balanced by websites from the kangaroo industry and the Australian government setting out the benefits of the industry and presenting a different narrative. There are no scientific societies (except where the conservation groups have scientific interests) devoted to the study of kangaroos.

ABORIGINAL DREAMING STORIES
A rich resource aimed at teachers and including several kangaroo stories as well as a great deal of other material.
www.teachers.ash.org.au/jmresources/dreaming/stories.html

AUSTRALIAN SOCIETY FOR KANGAROOS
This is the best organized of many societies aimed at the protection and conservation of kangaroos and is mainly dedicated to educating the public about kangaroo culling and the conservation status of different kangaroo species.
www.australiansocietyforkangaroos.org

AUSTRALIAN WILDLIFE MANAGEMENT SOCIETY
This is a largely scientific society dedicated to developing a science-based approach to wildlife management, including kangaroos.
www.awms.org.au

AUSTRALIAN WILDLIFE PROTECTION COUNCIL
This wild animal protection group is devoted mainly, but not exclusively, to the kangaroo.
www.awpc.org.au

DEPARTMENT OF FOREIGN AFFAIRS AND TRADE
This is part of this Australian ministry's About Australia website and seeks to set out a balanced view of the conservation status of kangaroos and the nature of the kangaroo industry.
www.dfat.gov.au/facts/kangaroos.html

DEPARTMENT OF SUSTAINABILITY, ENVIRONMENT, WATER, POPULATION AND COMMUNITIES
This is a government website concerned with native animals and specifically contains information concerned with the kangaroo industry and kangaroo culling.
www.environment.gov.au/biodiversity/wildlife-trade/wild-harvest/index.html

HOW THE KANGAROO GOT ITS POUCH
An Indigenous Australian storyteller recounts the Wiradjuri tale of how the kangaroo got its pouch. In Wiradjuri country (northwest New South Wales) kangaroo dreaming is largely associated with women.
www.youtube.com/watch?v=FdZytoa12NE

KANGAROO INDUSTRY ASSOCIATION OF AUSTRALIA
This is the umbrella website for a number of organizations and companies involved in different aspects of the kangaroo industry. It seeks to educate the public about the kangaroo industry and to promote its products.
www.kangaroo-industry.asn.au

MARSUPIAL SOCIETY OF AUSTRALIA
This is a small South Australian society devoted to the study of

marsupials and marsupial issues. It is more concerned with welfare issues than the scientific study of marsupials.
www.marsupialsociety.org/about.html

MARSUPIAL SOCIETY OF VICTORIA
This Victoria-based society combines a scientific approach with welfare issues.
www.vicmarsupial.org.au

NATIONAL KANGAROO PROTECTION COALITION
This is an alliance of 33 Australian animal welfare groups and some overseas groups promoting kangaroos and conservation. Other, smaller groups also exist, such as Stop Kangaroo Killing and the Kangaroo Protection Co-operative Ltd.
www.kangaroo-protection-coalition.com

THINKK
The Think Tank for Kangaroos is based at the University of Technology Sydney and is the premier centre for welfare-based kangaroo research in Australia.
www.thinkkangaroos.uts.edu.au

TREE-KANGAROO AND MAMMAL GROUP INC.
This is a Queensland-based group devoted to the preservation of tree-kangaroos in Australia. Groups such as the Tree Kangaroo Appreciation Society and the Tree Kangaroo Conservation Programme are devoted to preserving tree-kangaroo populations in Papua New Guinea.
www.tree-kangaroo.net

WILDLIFE PRESERVATION SOCIETY OF AUSTRALIA
The WSPA is the oldest and best-established organization devoted to the protection of Australian wildlife.
www.wpsa.org.au/index.html

Acknowledgements

In late 2008 my life took a curious turn when an unexpected phone call started a chain of events that nine months later found me living and working at Macquarie University in Sydney, Australia. Just over a year later I can honestly say that I have never regretted that move for one second. The really strange part of this story is that, although I had no plans to go to live in Australia, I had mentally inhabited Australia for two or three years in that I had just completed my book *Rossetti's Wombat: Pre-Raphaelites and Australian Animals in Victorian London*. In addition, when I moved to take up a post at the University of Lincoln in 2005, I had delivered an inaugural lecture entitled *The Kangaroo: England's National Symbol* and at least part of this book derives from work I did then. So this book has, in various conceptual forms, been around for a long time and it is a complete coincidence that it was written entirely in Australia where I can see kangaroos any day of the week by driving about an hour out of town.

I would like to thank my Vice-Chancellor, Professor Steven Schwartz, and my Provost, Professor Judyth Sachs, for bringing me to Macquarie and to Australia. I would also like to thank my colleagues Mark Gabbott, Janet Greeley and Stephen Thurgate for their enormously supportive welcome to me and all my colleagues in the Faculty of Arts whose good will and genuine warmth have made my first year in Australia a great deal easier and more pleasant than it might have been. Bill Stinson of Macquarie University Library provided me with some rare local history sources and Dr Shayne Williams of the Darug people advised on Indigenous culture. Nancy Cushing and Kevin Markwell of the University of Newcastle kindly gave me access to their unpublished work on boxing kangaroos. Carlene Kirvan's indefatigable work in pursuing picture permissions has been invaluable.

I thank my wife Kathryn who is now producing the most wonderful new series of paintings and linocuts which far outshine the quality of anything I ever manage to do.

The Feast of ss Martyrios and Marcianos the Notaries, 2011

Photo Acknowledgements

The author and publishers wish to express their thanks to the following sources of illustrative material and/or permission to reproduce it.

Photos Effy Alexakis: pp. 9, 10, 11, 12, 13, 28, 31, 34, 35, 36, 38, 39, 40, 42, 47, 55, 58, 63, 65, 68, 71, 73, 77, 88, 96, 147; photo Mark Appelt: p. 18 (top); photo aptronym, all rights reserved: p. 46; photo Ardea: p. 22; Art Gallery of New South Wales, Sydney: p. 41; © Australian Olympic Committee: p. 122; photos courtesy Australian War Memorial, Campbell, ACT: pp. 114 (foot), 115, 117, 118; from Thomas Bewick, *A General History of Quadrupeds*, 4th edition (Newcastle upon Tyne, 1800): p. 84; from the *Canberra Times* (2009): p. 49; from Marcel Cardillo and Adrian Lister, 'Evolutionary Biology: Death in the Slow Lane', *Nature*, CDXIX/440–441 (3 October 2002): p. 20; photo CityLibraries Townsville, Queensland: p. 50; Commonwealth Scientific and Industrial Research Organisation, Australia: p. 25 (top); from *Cornelis De Bruins Reizen Over Moskovie, Door Persie en Indie: Verrykt met Driehondert konstplaten, Vertoonende de beroemste lantschappen en steden, ook de byzondere dragten, beesten, gewassen en planten, die daer gevonden worden; Voor al Derzelver Oudheden, en wel voornamentlyk heel uitvoerig, die van het heerlyke en van oudts geheele werrelt door befaemde Hof Van Persepolis, By de Persianen Tchilminar genaemt; Alles door den Auteur zelf met groote naeukeurigkeit na't leven afgetekent, en noit voor dezen in't ligt gebragt* (Amsterdam, 1714): p. 69; photo Pauline Crawford © Northern Territory Library, Darwin (Pauline Crawford collection): p. 24; from Cornelis de Jode, *Speculum Orbis Terrae* (Antwerp, 1593): p. 71; Marianne Evers:

p. 111 (upper middle left); courtesy Fauna Productions: p. 98; photo © Jean-Paul Fererro/Auscape International: p. 22; photo Hedley Finlayson, from H. H. Finlayson, '*Caolprymnus campestris*, its Recurrence and Characters', *Transactions of the Royal Society of South Australia*, 56 (1932): p. 37; photo © Freder/2012 iStock International Inc.: p. 6; photo © Roger Garwood and Trish Ainslie 2012: p. 48; Ian Giles: p. 111 (upper middle right); from John Gould, *Mammals of Australia*, vol. II (London, 1863): pp. 9, 10, 11, 12, 13, 28, 31, 34, 35, 36, 38, 39, 40, 42, 47, 55, 58, 68, 73, 88, 96, 147; photo Jack Glover Gunn: p. 163; photo Lannon Harley (courtesy National Museum of Australia, Canberra): p. 127; courtesy Rolf Harris: p. 159; from John Hawkesworth, *An Account of the Voyages Undertaken by the Order of His Present Majesty for making Discoveries in the Southern Hemisphere, and successively Performed by Commodore Byron, Captain Wallis, Captain Carteret, and Captain Cook, in the 'Dolphin', the 'Swallow', and the 'Endeavour' . . .*, vol. III (London, 1773): pp. 82, 83; from John Hunter, *Birds & Flowers of New South Wales drawn on the spot in 1788, '89 & '90* (1788–90): p. 85; from *The Illustrated Australian News* (1 December 1893): p. 102; from the *Illustrated Australian News for Home Readers* (28 January 1874): p. 100; from *The Illustrated London News* (19 February 1887): p. 162; Bill Israel: p. 180; Athol Kelly: p. 111 (lower middle right and bottom right); artwork courtesy Ralph Kelly, Flags Australia: pp. 111 (bottom right image from Ralph Kelly's lecture 'Filibuster: The Century-long Flag Debate' at the 17th International Congress of Vexillology, Cape Town, 1997); from Josef Kořenský, *Obrazy z jižní polokoule* (Prague, 1902): p. 135; Library of Congress, Washington, DC (Prints and Photographs Division): pp. 119, 160, 179 (George Grantham Bain Collection); from *The Literary Magazine and British Review* (July 1790): p. 139; © Michael Long/NHMPL: p. 20; Lunn-Dyer and Associates: p. 111 (top right); photo Jason McCarthy: p. 116; photo Joseph McGlennon: p. 175; photo courtesy David Mallon: p. 167; photo G. Eric Matson: p. 119; photo Leonard John Matthews: p. 120; © Estate of Eileen Mayo: p. 131; *Melbourne Punch*, I (1855): p. 123; image courtesy of Michael Reid Gallery: p. 175; photo Mullins: p. 115; photos courtesy of Mitchell Library, State Library of New South Wales, Sydney, Australia: pp. 86, 139; photo Adam Monkhouse: p. 52; photo

Index